T0159007

TWO EXISTENTIAL
THEORIES OF
KNOWLEDGE

TWO EXISTENTIAL THEORIES OF KNOWLEDGE

EPISTEMIC PRAGMATISM
and
CONTEXTUALISM

JOSEPH W. LONG

TWO EXISTENTIAL THEORIES OF KNOWLEDGE
EPISTEMIC PRAGMATISM AND CONTEXTUALISM

iUniverse books may be ordered through booksellers or by contacting:

iUniverse
1663 Liberty Drive
Bloomington, IN 47403
www.iuniverse.com
1-800-Authors (1-800-288-4677)

ISBN: 978-1-5320-4137-2 (sc)
ISBN: 978-1-5320-4138-9 (e)

Library of Congress Control Number: 2018900719

Print information available on the last page.

iUniverse rev. date: 01/18/2018

Contents

ACKNOWLEDGMENTS

I AM ONCE AGAIN deeply indebted to many colleagues, professors, students, and friends. This work would not be possible without their generous contributions. Specifically, I wish to thank Charlene Haddock Seigfried, Donald Crosby, and Arthur Wayne Viney, from whom I learned so very much about the pragmatist philosophy of James and Dewey. I also wish to acknowledge (again) the late William L. Rowe, as well as Richard Kitchener and Jose Medina for generously sharing their expertise about the philosophy of Wittgenstein. I am forever indebted to William McBride and the late Calvin Schrag, who introduced me to the existentialist philosophies of Sartre, Camus, and Kierkegaard. Those philosophies have not only shaped my work but also my life. I owe a great debt of thanks to Paul B. Thompson, Joseph Margolis, and Hugh McDonald for generously sharing their own work with me, including manuscripts unpublished at the time of this writing, as well as to James Bohman, from whom I learned so much about the "neo-pragmatists", especially Robert Brandom. And I must thank Juli Thorson, whose undergraduate epistemology course set me upon this path many years ago.

I have also received munificent support from so many friends both inside and outside of philosophy. Thanks especially to Joe Tyson, who has always allowed me to indulge my need to philosophize, even on the golf course. Finally, I wish to thank my family. To my parents, Clarence and Mary Long, who cared for me during my unexpected extended illness, who always loved me and supported my journey, even if they didn't understand it, I will try to pay forward all of that love. To Don, Randy, Anthony, Patty, and Ted: thank you for your love, support, and friendship.

Finally, this book is dedicated to the memory of my sister, Sherrie, the most selfless person I've ever known, who typed out countless notes for me during the period of my illness, and to my nephew, Ryan, a creative, gentle compassionate man whose story was tragically cut short.

Sherrie Lynn Coloumbe 1963-2014

William Ryan Ledgerwood 1979-2017

INTRODUCTION

THE MOTIVATION FOR this project has been with me for a long time now. As a master's student, I found myself unsatisfied with the traditional foundationalist account of knowledge and although I discovered much to be admired in the coherentist paradigm, I was not convinced that epistemic coherentism represented a tenable theory of justification. This led me to explore the alternative epistemology of the later Wittgenstein and I spent more than a year in lost amazement, delightfully wondering the mysterious labyrinth of Wittgenstein scholarship. At the same time, I was enrolled in a seminar on the philosophy and psychology of William James and I became aware of some important commonalities between the two thinkers. Specifically, James and Wittgenstein held nontraditional theories of justification and unusual views on the noumenal. I explored these similarities in my thesis, in which I ultimately defended a version of Wittgensteinian contextualism. Along the way, I also began to notice some important differences.

My interest in these alternatives paradigms of justification intensified with my participation in a seminar entitled "Neo-Pragmatism." The course featured readings by classical pragmatists as well as such varied contemporary thinkers as Richard Rorty, Hilary Putnam, David Annis, William Alston, Robert Brandom, Donald Davidson, W. V. O. Quine, and Wilfrid Sellars. That seminar led me to the simple but important questions, *what do all of these thinkers have in common? What is it that makes the title "Neo-pragmatism" appropriate to all of them?* In my subsequent survey of literature, these names and others kept coming up again and again under the umbrella term, "neo-pragmatism", but I did not know why they should. It seemed to me that some of these thinkers held very different beliefs, epistemologically and metaphysically.

Eventually, under the guidance of my Ph.D. mentor and dissertation director, Charlene Haddock Seigfried (partly as a student in her seminar on the philosophy of John Dewey), I wrote a paper entitled, "Who's a Pragmatist?: Distinguishing Epistemic Pragmatism and Contextualism."[1] In this paper, published in the *Journal of Speculative Philosophy* in 2002, I promised to "attempt to define epistemic pragmatism"[2] and differentiate it from epistemic contextualism. I continued my attempts to flesh out these paradigms in my dissertation (Purdue University, 2005.)

But presently, twelve years after the writing of my dissertation, I find myself again unsatisfied and wanting to return to these unresolved epistemic problems. Although I do not disavow my earlier work, I believe that it is flawed because I was working under some latent and naïve assumptions. Most notably, in my 2002 article, I tried to

---

[1] "Who's a Pragmatist: Distinguishing Epistemic Pragmatism and Contextualism," The Journal of Speculative Philosophy, Volume 16, Number 1, 2002, pp. 39-49.

[2] ibid. 1.

define epistemic pragmatism according to three analytic criteria. I was approaching this distinction as an analytic philosopher and as an essentialist trying to find the necessary and sufficient conditions for epistemic pragmatism and contextualism. I now regard this aim as largely misguided. Pragmatism and contextualism are each broad families of theories that may elude clear categorization via necessary and sufficient conditions. In this present work, I believe it is more prudent to point out some important "family resemblances", general differentiating features which will help us to view pragmatism and contextualism more accurately and as distinct from other paradigms as well as from each other. It will also aid efforts to codify these so-called "neo-pragmatist" philosophers.

Another shortcoming of my earlier work was that my analytic approach limited my range of view to the Anglo-American tradition. In the last decade, I have become enamored with continental existentialist philosophy and I now realize that many of the objections that James, Dewey, and Wittgenstein (in particular) raised were existential ones. I hope that my present work will help build a bridge between the pragmatist, contextualist, and existentialist traditions.

CHAPTER ONE

I WISH TO BEGIN this book in much the same way
that Paul Moser began his 1986 anthology, *Empirical
Knowledge*[3], by distinguishing four of the leading
paradigms of epistemic justification and codifying them
according to their particular responses to the regress
problem of inferential justification. The paradigms of
justification I will focus on in this book will differ from
Moser's. While Moser includes epistemic infinitism, a view
which he attributes to Peirce, in his codification, he neglects
epistemic pragmatism, a paradigm which will be central to
this work.

I will explore each of these four paradigms (epistemic
foundationalism, epistemic coherentism, epistemic pragmatism,
and epistemic contextualism) in turn, along the way pointing
out important similarities between foundationalism and
coherentism (which I will call the traditional paradigms of
justification) and between pragmatism and contextualism
(which I will call the alternative paradigms.) This will also
involve an exploration into two important theories of first

---

[3]   Paul Moser. "Empirical Knowledge." 1986. Empirical
        Knowledge. Rowman & Littlefield, 1986. p. 7.

philosophy. I will show how the alternative paradigms are existentially superior to the traditional models. Finally, in this chapter, I will recount some popular arguments against foundationalism and coherentism respectively, provide an original argument against both, and demonstrate how the alternative paradigms spring from a more judicious and pertinent first philosophy.

SECTION 1.1: THE REGRESS PROBLEM AND FOUR EPISTEMIC PARADIGMS

One of the most obdurate problems in contemporary epistemology is the regress problem of inferential justification. What is inferential justification? By *inferential justification,* I simply mean justification that is reasoned from one or more other beliefs as premises to the *justificandum* belief as conclusion.[4] Inferentially justified beliefs need not *arise* inferentially. That is to say, beliefs which obtain this support do not have to be arrived at by deductive, inductive, or analogical methods. Rather, they simply must be able to trace their justification back to epistemically prior supporting beliefs in order to be inferential.[5] Inferential justification has been a staple and standard of justification throughout the history of epistemology. It is difficult, in fact, to imagine an epistemology that doesn't rely on inference, but inferential justification leads to a sticky problem.

---

[4]   Laurence Bonjour. "The Coherence Theory of Empirical Knowledge." 1976. Empirical Knowledge. Rowman & Littlefield, 1986. p. 117.

[5]   Bonjour, "Can Empirical Knowledge Have a Foundation?" 1978. Empirical Knowledge. Rowman & Littlefield, 1986. p. 97.

The regress problem of inferential justification is essentially this: Every belief *e* inferentially justifying a claim *c* must be supported by at least one further belief *f*; this belief *f* must likewise be inferentially supported by another belief *g* and so on like this, apparently *ad infinitum*. Of course, it seems to be of little justificatory value to derive a claim from a series of unjustified beliefs. Rather, a claim is *prima facie* justified only if the epistemically prior supporting beliefs are justified. (Claim *c* is justified only if belief *e* is justified; belief *e* is justified only if *f* is . . . and so on.) What threatens is "an infinite and apparently vicious regress of epistemic justification."[6] Justification (and hence, knowledge, since justification is a necessary condition for almost every conceivable theory of knowledge[7]) can never be had, for it can never even "get started."[8]

There are a number of ways to potentially handle the problem:

(1) One could maintain that the regress terminates in certain *empirically basic* beliefs – these are non-inferentially justified beliefs which are capable of carrying the load of empirical knowledge on their collective back;

---

[6] Bonjour, 1978. p. 97

[7] Gettier's paper cast doubt on the accepted notion that knowledge is (merely) a justified true belief; however, most epistemologists would still say that justification is a necessary condition for knowledge; see Edmund Gettier, "Is Justified True Belief Knowledge?" 1963. Empirical Knowledge. Rowman & Littlefield, 1986.

[8] Bonjour, 1978. p. 97.

(2)   one could maintain that while all justification is inferential, inferential justification is not linear, but in fact, circular or web-like;

(3)   one could maintain that the regress problem is completely averted because some beliefs are immediately justified or unjustified based upon the practical difference their veracity would make in our experience of and interaction with the world;

(4)   or one could maintain that the regress terminates in beliefs which are *contextually basic*. These are beliefs which lie "beyond being justified or unjustified"[9] and supply only contingent justification to the edifice of empirical knowledge.

These four possibilities represent (in a very basic way – I will elaborate further later in this chapter) the four leading paradigms of epistemic justification. They are epistemic foundationalism, epistemic coherentism, epistemic pragmatism, and epistemic contextualism respectively. It should be noted that this is not an exhaustive list; that is to say, these are not the only possible paradigms of justification. There are others. One theory, as Moser tells us, is infinitism. Infinitists deny that the regress of inferential justification is vicious and thereby allow for an infinite chain of justified beliefs. This has not been a popular view, but has been held by some. Most notably, Paul Moser attributes this view to Peirce.[10] I think it is difficult to pin down Peirce's response to the regress problem of inferential justification, but if Moser

---

9   Ludwig Wittgenstein. On Certainty. Edited by G. E. M. Anscombe and G.H. von Wright. New York: Harper, 1969. §359.

10   Paul Moser. "Empirical Knowledge." 1986. Empirical Knowledge. Rowman & Littlefield, 1986. p. 7.

is right, it adds even more tumult to Peirce's already blurred legacy in the history of pragmatism, the theory that he formulated in 1873, popularized in 1878, and perhaps denied or disavowed in 1910, writing in *Additament to the Article -- A Neglected Argument for the Reality of God,* "Thereupon I thought it high time to give my method a less distinguished designation; and I rechristened it pragmaticism."[11] Because of this controversy and because of Peirce's deliberate dissociation with pragmatism, I will not appeal to Peirce as a paradigm example of pragmatism in this book.

Another possible response to the regress problem is, of course, to deny that there is any way out. This would represent the paradigm of epistemic skepticism, a view maintained perhaps by Hume and certainly by Sextus Empiricus. In addition, there may be other, more positive responses which represent paradigms not yet established or little known. Nevertheless, the four responses enumerated above are the leading responses to the regress problem of inferential justification and represent the four paradigms that I will be considering in this work.

SECTION 1.2: FOUNDATIONALISM

Later in this chapter, I will present several seminal arguments against specific foundationalist projects and

---

[11]   C. S. Peirce, "Additament to the Article — A Neglected Argument for the Reality of God." The original article was published in The Hibbert Journal, A Quarterly Review of Religion, Theology, and Philosophy 7 (October 1908): 90-112, followed two years later by the "Additament" in 6.486490. The text can be found at the Peirce Project website at http://www. iupui.edu/~peirce/ep/ep2/headers/notes/note29.htm

an original argument against foundationalism generally, but first I think a brief exploration of foundationalism is necessary. Although I refer to foundationalism in this book as one of the paradigms of justification, it should not be assumed that foundationalism is a single and plenary view. A number of varied foundationalist projects have been advanced throughout the history of philosophy and more varied accounts are being advanced in the twenty-first century by thinkers such as John Greco. A kind of epistemic foundationalism was advanced by Plato and Aristotle, and by many of their Medieval descendants. The character, Socrates, in Plato's *Theaetetus,* defends a kind of foundationalism, insisting that the "'simple elements' are known even though they are not susceptible to further explanation."[12]

> Then, if we argue from the letters and syllables of which we have experience to other simples and compounds, we shall say that the letters or simple elements as a class are much more distinctly known than the syllables, and much more indispensable to a perfect knowledge of any subject; and if someone says that the syllable is known and the letter unknown, we shall consider that either intentionally or unintentionally he is talking nonsense[13]

A more decisive defense of foundationalism and arguably a more mature version is found in Aristotle's *Posterior Analytics.* He writes,

---

[12]   John Greco, Putting Skeptics in Their Place. Cambridge: Cambridge University Press, 2000. p. 109.

[13]   Plato, Theaetetus, 206b.

> Some people think that because you must understand the primitives there is no understanding at all; others that there is, but that there are demonstrations of everything. Neither of these views is either true or necessary . . ..

> We assert that not all understanding is demonstrative: rather, in the case of immediate items understanding is indemonstrable. And it is clear that this must be so; for if you must understand the items which are prior and from which the demonstration proceeds, and if things come to a stop at some point, then these immediates must be indemonstrable.[14]

But the ultimate form of foundationalism was that maintained by Descartes. In his *Meditations on First Philosophy* as well as the *Discourse on Method,* Descartes uses methodic doubt in order to find a firm and unshakeable foundation for all knowledge. From this most basic belief, the *cogito,* he builds up the edifice of empirical knowledge. This sort of project has been called *radical foundationalism.* It is essentially the view that certain basic beliefs (or in Descartes' case, a single belief) enjoys an epistemic immunity which springs from those beliefs' indubitability, incorrigibility, or irrevisability, and those *certain* foundations can inferentially support the rest of our knowledge.

Although it may be the most manifest type of foundationalist project, Cartesian radical foundationalism is certainly not the only sort of foundationalism. A more

---

14   Aristotle, Posterior Analytics, Book Alpha, Chapter 3.

moderate position held by such thinkers as Anthony Quinton, C. I. Lewis, and at times, Roderick Chisholm, maintains that epistemological reduction to indubitable or otherwise certain beliefs is not necessary for foundationalism. Chisholm writes,

> In many instances the answers to our questions will take the following form: 'What justifies me in thinking that I know a is F is the fact that it is evident to me that b is G.' For example, 'What justifies me in thinking that I know that he has that disorder is the fact that it is evident to me that he has those symptoms.'

Chisholm continues,

> We might try to continue *ad infinitum,* justifying each new claim that we elicit by still another claim. Or we might be tempted to complete a vicious circle: in such a case, having justified 'a is F' by appeal to 'b is G,' and 'b is G' by reference to 'c is H,' we would then justify 'c is H' by reference to 'a is F.' But if we are rational beings, we will do neither of these things. For we will find that our Socratic question leads us to a proper stopping place.[15]

---

15   Roderick Chisholm, Theory of Knowledge, 2nd edition. pp. 18-19.

These thinkers (Chisholm, Quinton, and Lewis) hold that empirically basic beliefs need only be *justified* in order to support higher order beliefs. Indubitability, incorrigibility, or irrevisability is not required. Laurence Bonjour writes that the central thesis of modest foundationalism

> is the claim that certain empirical beliefs possess a degree of epistemic warrant which does not depend, inferentially or otherwise, on the justification of other empirical beliefs, but is instead somehow immediate or intrinsic. It is these non-inferentially justified beliefs, the unmoved . . . movers of the epistemic realm, as Chisholm has called them, that constitute the foundation upon which the rest of empirical knowledge is alleged to rest.[16]

There seem to be two types of non-inferential justification available to modest foundationalists. Foundational beliefs might be self-justifying; these beliefs would not rely inferentially or otherwise on support from other beliefs or from non-belief sources, such as perception, sensation, or memory. A second and more common type of modest foundationalism is *givenism*. This is the view that the regress of inferential justification terminates with a given experience (which may be sensory or introspective), rather than with a belief. This brand of foundationalism is discussed most famously in Roderick Chisholm's seminal 1964 paper, "The

---

16   Bonjour, 1978. p. 95.

Myth of the Given,"[17] but has also been held by many in the twentieth century.

There may, in fact, be other possible forms of foundationalism which are lesser known or yet to be established. I am not concerned in this work with capturing or codifying every possible foundationalist project, but rather with painting a picture of epistemic foundationalism generally. For the purposes of this book, I will take epistemic foundationalism to be any of the family of theories that maintain that empirical knowledge requires non-inferentially justified beliefs that provide justification for all justified beliefs not among the foundations of knowledge.[18]

SECTION 1.3: COHERENTISM

The other leading theory of justification is epistemic coherentism. Coherentism is primarily a late 20th century view, but a mature form of coherentism was held as early as the 1930s by A. C. Ewing. In his book, *Idealism: A Critical Survey,* Ewing writes,

> The coherence principles provides the only rational justification for induction. The newer school of logicians admit that they have not succeeded in providing such a justification . . . .. But, if we assume that in any given case the hypothesis which comes

---

[17] Chisholm. "The Myth of the Given." 1964. Empirical Knowledge. Rowman & Littlefield, 1986.

[18] Moser, p. 4-5; see also David B. Annis, "A Contextualist Theory of Epistemic Justification," 1978. Empirical Knowledge. Rowman & Littlefield, 1986. p. 203.

nearest to making experience a coherent system is the one which ought to be accepted, then we have a principle by which we may easily justify the inductive process in general and any subordinate principles which it may require. We have arrived at a single principle again and can dispense with a plurality of unjustified assumptions. For obviously any principle really necessary for induction must be *ipso facto* one without which it would be impossible to make any coherent system of our experience, and all such assumptions could therefore be deduced from the principle of coherence alone.[19]

Coherentism has not traditionally been as popular as foundationalism as a response to the regress problem of inferential justification, but it's popularity has been growing in recent years. Partly due to important thinkers such as Keith Lehrer, Keith DeRose, and Laurence Bonjour, coherentism is presently enjoying its most ardent and widespread appeal. Even many non-coherentists in the twentieth-century, such as Wittgenstein and W. V. O. Quine, have recognized the importance of coherence to justification. Wittgenstein, for instance, writes, "It is not single axioms that strike me as obvious, it is a system in which consequences and premises give one another *mutual* support."[20]

Like foundationalism, coherentism is not any single

---

[19] A. C. Ewing. Idealism: A Critical Survey. London: 1934. pp. 247-8.

[20] Wittgenstein, On Certainty, §141.

theory or view, but rather a diverse family of theories. As Annis says, coherence theorists have rarely agreed about "what coherence is" or reached accord about "specifying the special system of statements" which are to be the criteria for such justification.[21] There seem to be at least three common types of coherentist theories. These are articulated nicely by Moser in his paper, "Empirical Knowledge," and can be found in demonstration in the works of Nicholas Rescher, Brand Blanshard, and Gilbert Harman. The first we may call *coherence as logical consistency.* This view, advocated by Rescher in his book, *The Coherence Theory of Truth* (1973), maintains that two beliefs are in a coherence relation and are therefore justified just in case it is logically possible for both beliefs to be true. This, of course, puts a very weak justification requirement on coherence. Another coherentist thesis, advocated by Blanshard in *The Nature of Thought,* is what Moser calls *coherence as logical implication.* Blanshard pronounces that two beliefs cohere just in case the truth of one logically guarantees the truth of the other. This puts a stronger requirement on coherence justification. A final sort of coherentist theory is discussed at length and finally defended by Harman in his 1973 book, *Thought.* Harman asserts that two beliefs cohere and are justified just in case one belief explains the truth value of the other. This seems to be the strongest kind of conherentist theory. Harman writes,

> Our 'premises' are all our antecedent beliefs;
> our 'conclusion' is our total resulting view.
> Our conclusion is not a simple explanatory
> statement but a more or less complete
> explanatory account. Induction is an attempt

---

[21]   Annis, p. 203.

to increase the explanatory coherence of our
view, making it more complete, less ad hoc,
more plausible.[22]

As with my discussion of foundationalism, the preceding is not intended to be an exhaustive codification of all possible coherentist theories. For example, it seems unclear how to best classify Lehrer's coherentism among these varieties. His theory may in fact represent a different and unique theory to any of these just mentioned. Further, there may be other possible coherentist views that are not widely held or are yet to be formulated. Although I will later take up arguments against each of the three varieties of coherentism which I have discussed, my principle goal is to probe coherentism generally. Therefore, for the purposes of this work I will satisfy myself with the following definition: I take epistemic coherentism to be any of the theories of justification which resolves to answer the regress problem of inferential justification by claiming that while all justification is inferential, it need not be linear, but may in fact be circular or web-like, where justified beliefs stand in a relationship of mutual support with one another.

Section 1.4: Pragmatism and Contextualism

Many trace the origin of pragmatism to Charles S. Peirce's 1878 paper, "How to Make Our Ideas Clear." But as I have suggested already, I think that this is a mistake. Or, more precisely, I think that if we take Peirce's seminal

---

[22]   Gilbert Harman. Thought. Princeton, NJ: Princeton University Press, 1973. p. 159.

article to be the plain beginning of pragmatism, we may be led into confusion rather than enlightenment about what pragmatism is. Certainly Peirce was key to the birth of pragmatism and an inspiration to William James. James acknowledges as much in his 1898 California address, "Philosophical Conceptions and Practical Results." But James also acknowledges the inspiration of other, more obscure figures, for example Shadworth Hodgson, who writes, "we are brought back once again to the *same practical common sense* of our starting point, the pre-philosophic attitude with which we originally confront the visible world."[23] In fact, Peirce advanced and amended his views later in his life, intentionally distancing himself from the view of James, announcing that he himself should not be classed as a "pragmatist" but rather a "pragmaticist." Because of this and because it is unclear how he responds to the regress problem of inferential justification, I will not be focusing on Peirce as my paradigm of pragmatism, but rather will choose as my example the mature work of William James and John Dewey.

I will not begin with a formal definition of pragmatism. Defining pragmatism, specifically epistemic pragmatism, is a great undertaking and will be one of the central aims of this book. In Chapter 2, I will attempt to elucidate pragmatism and to clearly distinguish it from contextualism. Presently, I wish to speak of epistemic pragmatism and epistemic contextualism in the broadest terms.

It should be emphasized that the term, "pragmatism" (and indeed, the term, "contextualism" also) refers to much

---

[23]   See Charlene Haddock Seigfried, "William James's Phenomenological Methodology," Journal of the British Society for Phenomenology, Volume 20, Number 1, January 1989.

more than simply a theory of knowledge. Pragmatism can rightly be described as a complete philosophical *Weltanschauung,* a whole and plenary view of the world and the human animal's relationship to it. Pragmatism is a complex organic system in which every part and parcel coheres with and relies upon every other. Thus it may be in some way inappropriate or illegitimate to partition off pragmatism's epistemology or metaphysics or ethics without talking about the whole. Nevertheless, I will for the most part, be focusing in this book on that narrow section of pragmatism that concerns the theory of knowledge. This I will call "epistemic pragmatism." And generally, I will use the term "pragmatism" in this work to refer specifically to epistemic pragmatism.

In his 1898 address, James compared his method of philosophy to that of a pathfinding hiker. Pragmatists are philosophers who wander and "who do not create anything beyond the marking of trails through the 'otherwise trackless forest of human experience.'"[24] James birthed what has since been called the *pragmatic principle* or *pragmatic rule.* According to this methodological rule, one should take two opposed "theses or positions and ask of each what 'conceivable practical consequence to anybody at any time or place' would follow if the thesis or position were regarded as true."[25] The consequences of the veracity of a belief determines its justification and if there is no *real* difference, then the question is discarded as merely 'specious' or 'verbal.'

Epistemic contextualism is a theory which holds that while there may be *logically foundational* beliefs, these

---

[24]   John E. Smith, Purpose and Thought: The Meaning of Pragmatism. New Haven: Yale University Press, 1978. p. 34.
       ibid. 35.

beliefs are not *epistemically foundational.* This distinction will be given greater color in Chapter 2. For now, let me say only that while there appear to be basic or foundational beliefs in contextualism, these contextually basic beliefs do not have the epistemic warrant that foundationalists purport to give them. Rather they are only *conditionally* justified or as Wittgenstein has said, they "lie beyond being justified or unjustified."[26] Epistemic contextualists also maintain that the requirements for justification of beliefs (including higher order beliefs) are relative to context. Wittgenstein, who I will focus on in this book as my paradigm of epistemic contextualism, calls this context the "language game." Some contemporary contextualists, including David Annis, have called it the "issue-context."[27]

Epistemic contextualism shares a great deal with epistemic pragmatism. Hilary Putnam recognizes this, writing, "The work of the later Wittgenstein 'bears affinities to American pragmatism even if he was not willing to be classed as a pragmatist."[28] Concerning just what affinities they share, Putnam says little, although he does explicitly maintain that Wittgenstein and the pragmatists share one central emphasis: "the primacy of practice." Indeed, there are a number of important commonalities between epistemic pragmatism and epistemic contextualism, and before distinguishing these paradigms from each other in Chapter 2, I would like to discuss the depth and scope of their affinity.

---

[26]   Wittgenstein, On Certainty. §359.

[27]   Annis, pp. 205-6.

[28]   Hilary Putnam, Pragmatism: An Open Question. p. 2.

Section 1.5: The Bridge Between Pragmatism and Contextualism

Clearly both contextualists and pragamtists emphasize the primacy of praxis. In "Pragmatist Metaphysics? Why Terminology Matters" (2001), Charlene Haddock Seigfried claims that pragmatists "express their . . . practice-centered perspective."[29] In her 1989 article, "William James's Phenomenological Methodology," Seigfried writes, "James consistently argues that philosophizing ought to begin in concrete experience, where 'every human being's practical life would begin.'"[30] She continues, quoting James, "The pragmatist clings to facts and concreteness, observes truth at work in particular cases . . .."[31]

In "The Meaning of Truth," James writes, "The whole originality of pragmatism, the whole point of it, is its use of the concrete way of seeing."[32] The primacy of practice can be seen nowhere clearer than in the pragmatic principle: ask what real difference a certain claim is supposed to make. Its truth is identical with its practical utility.

The centrality of praxis is also a trait manifest in epistemic contextualism. In his *Philosophical Investigations*,

---

[29] Charlene Haddock Seigfried, "Pragmatist Metaphysics? Why Terminology Matters", Transactions of the Charles S. Peirce Society, Winter 2001. Vol. XXXVII, Number 1, p. 13.

[30] Charlene Haddock Seigfried, "William James's Phenomenological Methodology," Journal of the British Society for Phenomenology, Volume 20, Number 1, January 1989. pp. 62-3.

[31] ibid. 63; see also William James, Pragmatism, p. 38.

[32] William James, "The Meaning of Truth," pp. 115-116; see also Seigfried, "William James's Phenomenological Methodology," p. 64.

Wittgenstein repeatedly stresses that "meaning lies in its use[,]"[33] and that we learn and teach "by means of *examples* and by *practice*[.]"[34] In his article, "A Contextualist Theory of Epistemic Justification," David B. Annis writes, "for S to be accountable for answering an objection, it must be a manifestation of a real doubt where the doubt is occasioned by *a real life situation*[,]"[35] and later, "[i]n considering the justification of beliefs we cannot neglect the actual social practices and norms of justification of a group."[36] In his groundbreaking book, *Wittgenstein and William James,* Russell B. Goodman claims that "James and Wittgenstein [not only] share views about specific topics, but that they share a set of commitments: . . . to the description of the concrete details of human life [and] to the priority of practice over intellect[.]"[37]

Another important similarity between pragmatism and contextualism is that both have a *social* element; justification depends to some degree on a social context or an epistemic community. Pragmatists and contextualists would agree that justification does not happen in a vacuum. It requires the social meeting of certain kinds of objections or truth tests. Indeed, this is perhaps the most salient and manifest trait of epistemic contextualism. Annis rejects foundationalism and coherentism, maintaining that both of these theories overlook important justificatory principles, such as the issue-context. "In particular," he writes, "the social nature

---

[33] Ludwig Wittgenstein, Philosophical Investigations, §197.

[34] ibid. §208.

[35] David B. Annis, "A Contextualist Theory of Epistemic Justification," p. 205; italics added for emphasis.

[36] ibid. 207.

[37] Russell B. Goodman, Wittgenstein and William James, Cambridge: Cambridge University Press, 2002. p. 5.

of justification cannot be ignored."[38] Wittgenstein concurs, writing, "Could one say 'I know the position of my hands with my eyes closed,' if the position I gave always or mostly contradicted the evidence of other people?"[39]

But social context is an important element in epistemic pragmatism as well. In "Context and Thought," Dewey discusses "the indispensability of context for thinking, and therefore for a theory of logic and ultimately of philosophy itself."[40] Later, he writes, "I know that there are many persons to whom it seems derogatory to link a body of philosophic ideas to the social life and culture of their epoch."[41] Dewey, then, criticizes those who "accept a dogma of immaculate conceptions of philosophical systems"[42] without taking into account their own social context.

A third important similarity between pragmatism and contextualism is that each strives for a coherent, holistic, and organic system of thought and takes into account natural organic and evolutionary models of justification and of discovery. Dewey carefully works out the organic approach of pragmatism in his 1909 article, "The Influence of Darwinism on Philosophy," and discusses the organic element of experience in "The Need for a Recovery of Philosophy" (1917): "experience is not identical with brain action: it is the entire organic agent-patient in all its interaction with the environment, natural and social."[43] In the same article, Dewey writes,

---

[38]   ibid. 212.

[39]   Wittgenstein, On Certainty, §502.

[40]   Dewey, "Context and Thought," p. 207.

[41]   ibid. 214.

[42]   ibid. 214.

[43]   Dewey, "The Need for a Recovery of Philosophy," p. 58.

When Descartes and others broke away from medieval interests, they retained as commonplaces its intellectual apparatus: Such as, knowledge is exercised by a power that is extra-natural and set over against the world to be known. Even if they had wished to make a complete break, they had nothing to put as knower in the place of the soul. It may be doubted whether there was any available empirical substitute until science worked out the fact that physical changes are functional correlations of energies, and that man is continuous with other forms of life, and until social life had developed an intellectually free and responsible individual as its agent.[44]

Contextualists agree. In his notes which would posthumously become the book *On Certainty,* Wittgenstein writes, "When we first begin to *believe* anything, what we believe is not a single proposition, it is a whole system of propositions. (Light dawns gradually over the whole.)"[45] Wittgenstein makes similar statements at §102, 144, and 225 of *On Certainty,* and discusses the *evolution* of the coherent system of knowledge at §63, 225, and 336. In fact, he writes that even the foundations of knowledge evolve: "When language-games change, then there is a change in concepts, and with the concepts the meanings of words change."[46]

Related to the holistic and organic nature of knowledge

---

44   ibid. 56.

45   Wittgenstein, On Certainty, §141-2.

46   ibid. §65.

in pragmatism and contextualism is the fact that in both of these paradigms knowledge is contingent and dynamic. Language-games change with time[47], and with them, the rules of justification change. Knowledge itself changes; it is not as Descartes imagines it – static and immutable. One reason knowledge claims change is that language-games become more and less important through time. Wittgenstein writes, "If we imagine the facts otherwise than as they are, certain language-games lose some of their importance, while others become important. And in this way there is an alteration . . . ."[48]

Furthermore, new language-games are continually coming into existence. Putnam writes, "Human beings are self-surprising creatures; we have always created new language-games, and we shall continue to create new language-games . . . ."[49]

In "Pragmatism and Radical Empiricism," James stresses the dynamic nature of pragmatic truth: "The truth of any idea is not a stagnant property in it. Truth *happens* to an idea. It *becomes* true, is *made* true by events."[50] Again: "Its veracity *is* in fact an event, a process . . . ."[51] This is made more clear in Seigfried's 1990 book, *William James's Radical Reconstruction of Philosophy.* There, Seigfried writes,

> Thus, to say that something is true is to say that it is satisfactory, even on the correspondence model of truth, as long as the scope of such satisfaction is kept in mind and not confused

---

[47] ibid. §256.

[48] ibid. §63.

[49] Putnam, Pragmatism: An Open Question, p. 32.

[50] James, "Pragmatism and Radical Empiricism," p. 312.

[51] ibid. 311.

with just any satisfaction anyone happens to have at the time. Given this analysis of the relationship of objective truth to subjective satisfaction, to continue to claim that truth consists in a static relation of idea to object, leaving out the whole notion of a possible or actual satisfactory working or leading which constitutes the pragmatic account, is to prefer a truth theory based on unexamined assumptions to an account grounded in experience. Absolutely objective truth can be claimed only by abandoning any attempt at relating it to concrete experience.[52]

The fact that pragmatism and contextualism view knowledge as dynamic rather than static clearly differentiates these paradigms from the traditional paradigms of epistemic justification, foundationalism and coherentism. In fact, both pragmatists and contextualists take care in separating themselves from the foundationalist tradition. In his 1996 article, "Pragmaticism is an Existentialism?", Kenneth L. Ketner argues that for pragmatists such as Peirce, "life is an experiment, with nothing guaranteed in advance and no sure path except to continue experimenting, correcting our errors as best we can as we push toward future interpretations. That is hardly the stance of a foundationalist, whether of the Cartesian or the sense-datum variety."[53] In her book, *William James's Radical Reconstruction of*

---

[52] Seigfried, William James's Radical Reconstruction of Philosophy, p. 314.

[53] Kenneth L. Ketner, "Pragmaticism is an Existentialism?" Frontiers in American Philosophy, Volume 2, 1996. p. 105.

Philosophy, Seigfried claims that "Just as Wittgenstein and Heidegger later rediscovered, the process of searching for foundations [for the pragmatist] becomes itself the issue, and the very thoroughness of the attempt to establish an unproblematic foundation provokes reflections which lead to radically reconceptualizing how we appropriate the world."[54] In *Wittgenstein and William James,* Russell Goodman explicitly sets out that among the commitments shared by Wittgenstein and James is the whole hearted commitment to "anti-foundationalism."[55] In addition to the primacy of practice, social justification, the organic and holistic nature of knowledge, and the dynamic (as opposed to static) nature of knowledge, epistemic pragmatism and epistemic contextualism also share an emphasis on picturesque language[56] and conceptual frameworks. But more importantly, pragmatism and contextualism share a deep-seated and stalwart affinity which makes the title "existential epistemologies" appropriate to both. Both pragmatists and contextualists take their philosophical starting point to be a human being's "lived situation."

---

[54]   Charlene Haddock Seigfried, William James's Radical Reconstruction of Philosophy. Albany: State University of New York Press, 1990. p. 3.

[55]   Russell B. Goodman, Wittgenstein and William James, Cambridge: Cambridge University Press, 2002. p. 5.

[56]   see Wittgenstein's On Certainty, §10 as well as his Philosophical Investigations; see also Seigfried's "Vagueness and the Adequacy of Concepts: In Defense of William James's Picturesque Style," Philosophy Today, Winter 1982, pp. 360-362.

SECTION 1.6: EXISTENTIAL EPISTEMOLOGIES

I have stated that pragmatists and contextualists share an emphasis on one's "lived situation," but in this section, I wish to explore the depth of this commitment. It is my claim that pragmatists, contextualists, and existentialists share a crucial *choice* regarding skepticism, and that in fact, these three schools share a unique first philosophy, which is wholly distinct from and incommensurable with the first philosophy which has dominated throughout the great majority of the history of western philosophy.

A hypothetical epistemologist might maintain that the difference between foundationalists and coherentists on one hand and pragmatists and contextualists on the other is that the former take the threat of skepticism seriously while the latter do not. The Cartesian project they might say, exemplifies the foundationalists respect for the problem of skepticism. Because pragmatists and contextualists refuse to engage in these sorts of projects, he might continue, these alternative paradigms of justification simply slight skepticism, but in this, our imaginary interlocutor is mistaken. Pragmatists, contextualists, and existentialists all take skepticism seriously, but they do not respond to it in the way that traditional epistemologists do. At the beginning of *The Myth of Sisyphus,* Albert Camus writes, "There is but one truly serious philosophical problem, and that is suicide. Judging whether life is or is not worth living amounts to answering the fundamental question of philosophy."[57] Here, Camus is taking skepticism extremely seriously. If our world, our life, remains an absurd riddle with no answers

---

[57]   Albert Camus, The Myth of Sisyphus, New York: Vintage International, Translated by Justin O'Brien, 1983. p. 3.

to be found, then what can we do? We can commit suicide or live in nihilism, or perhaps we can make another *choice*. The way out of skepticism for the existentialist is to make a choice. Perhaps it is an absurd choice.[58] Perhaps, as the foundationalists would say, it is an unjustified choice, but it

---

[58] "Absurd" is an important and technical term (though poetically described) for Camus. What follows is a set of definitions of "absurd" in Camus' own poetic words, followed by a philosophical interpretation of the term. Camus writes, "in a universe suddenly divested of illusions and lights, man feels an alien, a stranger. His exile is without remedy since he is deprived of the memory of a lost home or the hope of a promised land. This divorce between man and his life, the actor and his setting is properly the feeling of absurdity." (The Myth of Sisyphus, p. 6.) Again: "The discomfort in the face of man's own inhumanity, this incalculable tumble before the image of what we are, this 'nausea,' as a writer of today calls it, is also the absurd. Likewise the stranger who at certain seconds comes to meet us in a mirror, the familiar and yet alarming brother we encounter in our own photographs is also the absurd." (p. 15) "But what is absurd is the confrontation of this irrational and the wild longing for clarity whose call echoes in the human heart. The absurd depends as much on man as on the world. For the moment it is all that links them together." (p. 21) "If I see a man armed only with a sword attack a group of machine guns, I shall consider his act to be absurd. But it is so solely by virtue of the disproportion between his intention and the reality he will encounter, of the contradiction that I notice between his true strength and the aim he has in view." (p. 29) The Cambridge Dictionary of Philosophy, edited by Robert Audi, interprets the absurd as "the confrontation between ourselves – with our demands for rationality and justice – and an 'indifferent universe.'" (Entry by Robert C. Solomon; Second Edition, p. 116.)

is a choice we must make, or else sit on the side of the road wagging our thumbs with Sextus Empiricus.

Pragmatists and contextualists escape skepticism in the very same way that existentialists do – they make a positive choice. This choice may not be epistemically warranted, but it is necessary. In response to a skeptical challenge, Wittgenstein writes, ". . . somewhere I must begin with non-doubting; and that is not, so to speak, hasty but excusable . . .."[59] Again, he writes, ". . . somewhere I must begin with an assumption or a decision."[60] In *Pragmatism: An Open Question,* Hilary Putnam recognizes that pragmatists agree that "ceasing to believe anything at all is not a real human possibility."[61] Pragmatists and contextualists accept that part of our human condition or our "lived situation" is that we have only a limited perspective on the world and finite mental and sensory instruments to construct our picture of it. To listen to our senses and to mostly believe their testimony, to trust our experience of the world is the only viable existential choice if we are to live a meaningful human life. Pragmatists, contextualists, and existentialists do take skepticism seriously. But unlike foundationalists and coherentists, who remain in limbo looking for justification that may never be found, pragmatists, contextualists, and existentialists have opted to *choose* anti-skepticism (once again, not because this is warranted, but because it is necessary for living.) The alternative is simply *Waiting for Godot.*

Bertrand Russell views this 'anti-skeptical' decision as giving in to skepticism. He charges that pragmatism is a

---

[59] On Certainty, §150.

[60] ibid. §146.

[61] Pragmatism: An Open Question, p. 58.

theory which "deprives us of anything stable in which to believe, and [this makes pragmatism] in the end…profoundly and irresponsibly skeptical: The skepticism embodied in pragmatism is that which says, 'Since all beliefs are absurd, we may as well believe what is most convenient.' A pragmatist such as James, Russell continues, holds that in any context, including science, we should believe whatever gives us satisfaction."[62] This, I believe, is a gross misrepresentation of the pragmatic principle, and I will defend pragmatism against this charge in Chapter 2.

SECTION 1.7: PRAGMATIST AND CONTEXTUALIST FIRST PHILOSOPHY

Because of the way that pragmatists, contextualists, and existentialists answer the threat of skepticism, and because of the way they focus on the human animal's "lived situation," it is fair to refer to all of these schools as a kind of *humanism*. In fact, Sartre and James explicitly claim that their philosophy is a kind of humanism. (Interested readers should see Sartre's famous article, "Existentialism as a Humanism," and James's "The Essence of Humanism" and "Pragmatism and Humanism" as well as Patrick Dooley's book, *Pragmatism as Humanism: The Philosophy of William James.)* Wittgenstein's philosophy is also clearly one "with a human face."[63] In this section, I will show not only that pragmatists, contextualists, and existentialists are all humanists. (This much I now take to be manifest.) I will further attempt to illustrate the depth of their commitment

---

[62]   Russell B. Goodman, *Wittgenstein and William James*, Cambridge: Cambridge University Press, 2002. p. 13

[63]   see Putnam's 1990 book, *Reality with a Human Face*.

to humanism, showing that each shares a unique paradigm of first philosophy which takes as its logical starting point the human animal's "lived situation."

The first thing I wish to do in this section is define what I mean by a paradigm of first philosophy, for it may not be obvious. Professor Hugh McDonald is, at the time of my writing, working on an exciting book, which explores in depth paradigms of first philosophy. McDonald defines a "first philosophy" as the starting point of a philosophical system; it is that point at which one cannot go deeper without falling into an infinite regress. No knowledge claims or systems of philosophy are paradigm-free; all subscribe to a first philosophy. A first philosophy is not necessarily the first question that we ask. It is logically foundational, not epistemically. McDonald writes, "We may come to it last in learning, but it is logically prior as the ground of knowledge, the basis for all knowledge."[64] McDonald is careful to note that first philosophy is logically distinct from ontology, even though Aristotle and Descartes refer to ontology or metaphysics as "first philosophy." McDonald writes,

> Thus, for Aristotle, key terms must refer back to the universal ground, being. We have already seen how knowledge relates to being. For Aristotle, nature is also a type of being. Cause has being or a mode of being, while quantities and numbers refer back to being. Even logic, though formally empty, refers back to principles of being. Truth is the truth of being. Language was not a world unto itself, an incomprehensible "speaking

---

[64] Hugh McDonald, "System and Paradigm," p. 14.

in tongues" as it were, but as a basis through intending being. We speak about what 'is' for Aristotle. In sum, then, being is the central term in a cluster of key philosophic terms.[65]

Throughout the majority of the history of western philosophy, philosophers have taken the ontological as their logical starting point, their paradigm of first philosophy. Foundationalists and coherentists have clearly done so. But some original and innovative thinkers have taken other starting points. Karl Otto-Apel and Hugh McDonald disagree concerning the number of different paradigms of first philosophy that have existed throughout the history of philosophy. Otto-Apel differentiates three, while McDonald claims there are four. It is not relevant to my project to settle this issue, and I will not spend excessive time or space attempting to resolve this conflict. Rather, I wish only to note that there is more than one paradigm of first philosophy (that Aristotle's is not the only possible one), and no matter how many different paradigms there are, pragmatists, contextualists, and existentialists share a first philosophy that is distinct from Aristotle's traditional paradigm of first philosophy in which all things begin and end with Being. So, what is logically first for pragmatists, contextualists, and existentialists? *Living.* The meaningful experience of one's lived situation is more basic to pragmatists, contextualists, and existentialists than even Being or ontology. Sartre says that what all existentialists "have in common is simply the fact that *existence* comes before *essence* – or, if you will, that we must begin from the subjective . . ..

---

[65]   ibid. 15.

There is at least one being whose existence comes before its essence, a being which exists before it can be defined by any conception of it. That being is man, as Heidegger has it, the human reality. What do we mean by saying that existence precedes essence? We mean that man first of all exists, encounters himself, surges up in the world – and defines himself afterwards. If man as the existentialist sees him is not definable, it is because to begin with he is nothing. He will not be anything until later, and then he will be what he makes of himself.[66]

Pragmatists and contextualists begin with the subjective; for them existence precedes essence.

Although she does not frame the issue in terms of paradigms of first philosophy, no one articulates pragmatism's radical break with the ontological starting point better than Charlene Haddock Seigfried. In her 1990 article, "The Pragmatist Sieve of Concepts: Description Versus Interpretation," Seigfried writes,

pragmatism has sometimes been categorized as a version of realism and sometimes as idealism. But the originality of pragmatism cannot be fully grasped without recognizing that it is neither, because its analysis of concrete human experience rejects the metaphysical

---

[66] Jean-Paul Sartre, "Existentialism is a Humanism," Existentialism from Dostoevsky to Sartre, edited by Walter Kaufman. Cleveland, Meridian Books, 1956. pp. 289-290.

assumptions on which the distinction is based.[67]

In "Pragmatist Metaphysics? Why Terminology Matters,"[68] Seigfried describes pragmatists as "anti-essentialist" and discusses "pragmatist's emphatic assertions that metaphysics was the problem, not the solution."[69] She writes, "The centuries-long philosophical efforts to develop a metaphysics was considered by them at least a distraction from the concrete concerns of everyday life and at most a tragic detour away from everything that gives value and meaning to life."[70] And finally, in her book, *William James's Radical Reconstruction of Philosophy*[71], she writes,

Already in James's time, his account, like Schiller's and Dewey's, was criticized for emphasizing the subjective side of truth to the exclusion of the objective. His response is just as cogent today as then. The charge of subjectivism can be sustained only by clinging to the dogmatic view of reality

---

67 Charlene Haddock Seigfried, "The Pragmatist Sieve of Concepts: Description versus Interpretation," The Journal of Philosophy, Volume LXXXVII, Number 11, November 1990, p. 585.

68 Charlene Haddock Seigfried, "Pragmatist Metaphysics? Why Terminology Matters," Transactions of the Charles S. Peirce Society, Winter 2001, Volume XXXVII, Number 1, p. 13.

69 ibid. 13-14.

70 ibid. 13-14.

71 Seigfried, William James's Radical Reconstruction of Philosophy. Albany, NY: State University of New York Press, 1990.

characteristic of rationalism, which was already refuted by him. Not James, but Descartes, Hume, and Kant had relegated reality to the sidelines, making it wait upon experiential evidence to usher it back into the court of philosophic discourse. Any claims appealing to or designating 'reality' as the object or source of experience had either to be strictly derived from such experience or openly postulated as a belief. In his critical reconstruction of the flux of experience James drew out the radical consequences of such an experiential starting point."[72]

Pragmatists and contextualists share deep affinities with existentialists. Charlene Haddock Seigfried tells us that "James's criterion for philosophy is an engaged understanding and transformation of the human condition." This is an "existentialist understanding of philosophy as vocation . . ."[73] Kenneth Ketner abruptly expresses that "pragmaticism is an existentialism."[74] One trait that all of these groups share is their "recognition of the reality of persons: acting, choosing, suffering, living, searching, interpreting, dying beings."[75] What matters is our human

72 ibid. 311.

73 Seigfried, William James's Radical Reconstruction of Philosophy. Albany, NY: State University of New York Press, 1990. p. 4.

74 Kenneth L. Ketner, "Pragmaticism is an Existentialism?" Frontiers in American Philosophy, Volume 2, 1996. p. 105.

75 ibid. 107. Here, Ketner is discussing primarily the affinities between Peirce and the existentialists.

life. Camus writes, "To two men living the same number of years, the world always provides the same number of experiences. It is up to us to be conscious of them. Being aware of one's life, one's revolt, one's freedom, and to the maximum, is living, and to the maximum."[76] Wittgenstein recognizes this aspect of William James's work, remarking in 1929 that "James was a good philosopher because he was a real human being."[77] Camus ends "The Myth of Sisyphus," writing, "The preceding merely defines a way of thinking. But the point is to live."[78]

In this section, I have argued that pragmatists and contextualists share deep affinities with existentialism. Specifically, pragmatists and contextualists answer the threat of skepticism in the same unique manner and they share a first philosophy that starts from the real, concrete experience of one's lived situation. Because of these deep affinities, I believe we are justified in referring to epistemic pragmatism and contextualism as "existential epistemologies." In the remainder of this chapter, I will attempt to show why I think the existential epistemologies are, in some important ways, superior to the traditional paradigms of justification, foundationalism and coherentism.

---

[76] Albert Camus, "The Myth of Sisyphus" The Myth of Sisyphus and Other essays, Translated by Justin O'Brien. New York: Vintage Books, 1991. p. 62-63.

[77] Russell B. Goodman, Wittgenstein and William James, Cambridge: Cambridge University Press, 2002. p. 172.

[78] Albert Camus, "The Myth of Sisyphus" The Myth of Sisyphus and Other essays, Translated by Justin O'Brien. New York: Vintage Books, 1991. p. 65.

SECTION 1.8: SEMINAL OBJECTIONS TO FOUNDATIONALISM

In Section 1.2, I distinguished several types of foundationalist projects. The most conspicuous brand of foundationalism is the radical foundationalism of Descartes. In his *Meditations on First Philosophy* as well as in *The Discourse on Method,* Descartes uses methodic doubt in hopes of finding an ultimately foundational and indubitable belief. On these unshakeable foundations, he hopes to build his philosophy. But Descartes' project was unsuccessful. The critique of his foundationalism is generally two-fold: (1) Because of the ultimate rigor of his own method of doubt (which includes such efficient instruments as the dream argument and the evil demon) it seems quite problematic that any belief, even his intimation, *cogito ergo sum,* could in fact enjoy the status of indubitability. (2) Even assuming the knowledge of this or any other similarly basic belief, can we, from this belief alone, infer justification for our higher order beliefs? It seems not. Keeping Descartes' project in mind, where could one possibly go from *I am a thinking thing* without even utilizing logic or mathematical reasoning? There are other important criticisms as well; for instance, is an *indubitable belief necessarily a true belief?* It does not seem to follow logically that if I cannot doubt that p, p must be true. Even the most unshakeable belief might be false. A. J. Ayer writes, "There will not be a formal contradiction in saying both that the man's state of mind is such that he is absolutely sure that a given statement is true, and that the statement is false."[79] For reasons such as these, the hope for a Cartesian project in epistemology has been all but lost.

---

[79]   A. J. Ayer. The Problem of Knowledge, 1956. p. 19.

But, as I maintained earlier in this book, this sort of radical epistemological reduction to indubitable or otherwise certain beliefs is not necessary for a theory of justification to be classed as foundationalism. Modest foundationalists may simply claim that empirical knowledge requires non-inferentially justified beliefs which provide justification for all justified beliefs not among the foundations of knowledge.[80] In Section 1.2, I distinguished two kinds of non-inferential justification which seem to be available to modest foundationalists: (A) Foundational beliefs could be self-justifying, that is, foundational beliefs would not rely inferentially or otherwise on support from other beliefs or from non-belief sources, such as sensation or memory; or (B) foundational beliefs may be *given* via non-belief experiences (sensation, memory, etc..) Perhaps such a belief as "I see a red pen on the table" is *given* in just this way. There are a number of seminal arguments against modest epistemic foundationalism of types (A) and (B). I will present only the strongest here:

I. Moser and Bonjour both consider the following to be the most formidable argument against type (A) foundationalism: There can never really be a non-inferentially justified belief because one would only hold that this belief is justified if it has a certain feature, namely epistemic reliability or *truth-conduciveness*. (I will call this feature F.) Therefore, justification is contingent upon a belief's having feature F or being of the kind F. Let's look at how this belief is justified:

(i)   I have a belief that p has feature F (epistemic reliability.)
(ii) Beliefs having feature F are likely to be true.

---

[80]   see Moser, pp. 4-5 and Annis, p. 203.

(iii) Thus, my belief that p is likely to be true.

Such justification is obviously inferential and therefore, the belief that p is not foundational.

II. Laurence Bonjour articulates the problems with type (B) foundationalism very well. What follows then relies heavily on the reasoning he lays out in his 1976 article, "The Coherence Theory of Empirical Knowledge," and his 1978 article, "Can Empirical Knowledge Have a Foundation?", some of which I will paraphrase. The first problem for this theory is that it seems *prima facie* that the criticism to type (A) foundationalism will extend to type (B) as well, for they both would likely need something like feature F to be justified. However, type (B) foundationalism – which includes epistemic intuitionism and the theory of cognitive givenism – has been more prominent than type (A). In fact, Bonjour claims that "it is so venerable that it deserves to be called the standard foundationalist solution to the problem in question."[81]

The central notion of type (B) foundationalism is essentially this: " . . . basic beliefs are justified by reference not to further *beliefs,* but rather to states of affairs in the world which are 'immediately apprehended' or 'directly presented' or 'intuited.'"[82]

Thus, there are three items present at the foundation of epistemic justification for the foundationalist: a belief (that p), a state of affairs in the world, and an apprehension of that state of affairs. The questions before us now are *What is the nature of this apprehension?* and *Given its nature, is it capable of justifying our belief that p?* Different foundationalists

---

[81] Bonjour, 1978, p. 106.

[82] ibid. 106.

have responded in different ways to the first question. Lewis argues that the apprehensions are private cognitive states apprehended with certainty,[83] while Quinton asserts that the givens are not cognitive, but in fact states of affairs in the world.[84] Unfortunately for the foundationalist, both Lewis' view and Quinton's view have great epistemic problems: If the given is simply a cognitive state, then it is by its very nature private and subjective. It is most difficult to see how a subjective experience (like a perception or a memory) concerning a state of affairs in the world external to minds could be justified without making a kind of pragmatic leap. (In Chapter 2, I will discuss how pragmatists resolve this problem.) However, if the given is not a cognitive state, then how is it capable of offering justification to our beliefs? No matter what the nature of these givens, there is a substantial problem. Bonjour puts the dilemma well when he writes,

> [I]f [our] intuitions or immediate apprehensions are construed as cognitive, then they will be both capable of giving justification and in need of it themselves; if they are non-cognitive, then they do not need justification but are also incapable of providing it. This, at bottom, is why epistemological givenness is a myth.[85]

It is simple enough to see how a justified apprehension of the state of affairs that p could justify a corresponding belief. What is problematic is how this original apprehension

---

[83] ibid. 106-7.

[84] ibid. 107.

[85] ibid. 109.

could be justified without appealing to a further intuition or apprehension. Chisholm's answer is that these foundational apprehensions justify themselves.[86] But what does this mean – that our internal images or experience or sense data are justified, or that a belief about a state of affairs external to our minds is justified, or something else altogether?

We might put this another way: A belief can be either of the *internal* or *external* variety. An internal belief might be one like *I have a headache,* where the feeling that one has a headache is identical to one's *actually having* a headache. Perceptions can also give us an internal belief: *I am seeing a red pen on the table* (where to see means merely to have a certain sense impression.) An external belief might be one like *There is a red pen on the table* (this belief is about state of affairs in the actual world, not simply a sensory perception in our minds.) We will see later how the pragmatist's repairing of the distinction between appearance and reality will make many epistemic problems like this one easier to work through. The internal belief seems to be of little import to the foundationalist because she requires more justification to know that her senses are not deceiving her. In other words, her external belief is not inferable from the internal belief. The external world to which we are referring may not match up with her internal justified belief. So, the latter view (that the apprehension is a justified belief about the world external to minds) seems simply to be false because of the objection to the former.

If, instead, these apprehensions are non-cognitive (and therefore objective), then the need for justification is obviated, but it becomes quite problematic as to how a believer could justify a foundational belief is she is not

---

[86]   Chisholm, "The Myth of the Given," 1964, pp. 55-7.

in cognitive possession of the state of affairs which give justificatory power to that belief.

A final possibility for foundationalism comes via an *externalist* approach to the possibility of knowledge. Externalism is a position in which while knowledge requires a true justified belief, it is not necessary that the person for whom the belief is justified be in cognitive possession of either the justifying evidence or the truth of the proposition. In this book, I will be assuming an internalist approach to the possibility of knowledge. Although this is a presupposition, I do not believe it is without warrant. I believe externalist theories of knowledge are inadequate because they allow for knowledge without the knowledge of whether or not one has knowledge, and I think this is contrary to what is meant by the word "knowledge." Let me demonstrate: If one had a justified belief which *happened* to be true (although the believer didn't *know* it to be true), then he would have knowledge. However, if this belief *happened* to be false, then the believer would not have knowledge. Thus, a belief which has a very high level of justification might turn out *not* to be knowledge, while a belief with much lesser justification might indeed be knowledge. This does not seem to fit well with what we mean by knowledge because the believer who has knowledge and the believer who does not have knowledge seem to be in the same epistemic position.

Section 1.9: An Original Objection to Foundationalism

In the previous section, I presented several seminal objections to epistemic foundationalism. In this section,

I wish to provide a new objection inspired by continental Idealism.

Let's begin by making a distinction between two forms of empirical justification. I will call these *soft* and *hard justification*. I will argue that for the foundationalist, the soft form is untenable because it does not allow for access to truth; the hard form is unsuccessful because it will be impossible for (many) empirical beliefs to obtain such justification. Again: the soft form fails because *truth* is inaccessible; the hard form fails because *justification* is inaccessible. This argument does rest on an important assumption, although it is one that is commonly held by foundationalists: namely, that empirical knowledge consists, minimally, of a true justified belief. The Gettier-problem, or the problem of the necessary and sufficient conditions for empirical knowledge motivates an attempt to find additional necessary conditions for knowledge, but few epistemologists in the western tradition would argue that these criteria are not at least necessary for knowledge.

Most foundationalists are fallibilists, that is to say, they believe that a justified belief could in fact be false. But what kind of justified belief? I will call justification to the point of certainty *hard justification*, and any justification short of that *soft justification*. Now consider the following statement: *There is a red pen on the table.*

For an advocate of hard justification, this statement would be justified just in case (1) she has a belief that there is a red pen on the table, and (2) she has enough evidence to say with *certainty* that there is in fact a red pen on the table. For the *soft justificationist,* the same statement will be justified just in case (1) he has a belief that there is a red pen on the table, and (2) he has some evidence which makes this belief appear likely to be true.

But justification for the soft justificationist (although intimate to) is conceptually and epistemically independent of truth. The problem is (for the soft justificationist) that while one may be quite capable of reaching justified beliefs, we are not capable of saying with any additional certainty whether or not these beliefs are true, and of course, justified beliefs may in fact be false. Further, if truth is to be found, it seems evident that it must be as a result of justification. How else could we *find truth?* But the soft justificationist can have a justified belief the truth of which is in question. How then could one know whether or not one has knowledge? And of course, knowing that one has knowledge is a requirement of an internalist account of knowledge.

Hard justification is equally problematic. Although such justification may be logically possible, it is doubtful that we have very many beliefs (or in fact, any external empirical beliefs) which could meet such a rigorous standard. (Remember: an external belief is a belief about the world external to minds. Such a belief as *I have a headache* would not qualify as external since *having a headache* and *merely thinking I have a headache* are identical. In such an example, truth and justification are not epistemically independent.) It seems one could hardly reach such justification through perception. There are many reasons why a justified belief about an external empirical statement such as *There is a red pen on the table* can, in fact, be false: Perhaps the individual for whom the belief is justified has forgotten that he is wearing red-tinted contacts and the pen is actually white; perhaps he is looking at a pencil that looks like a pen; perhaps he is hallucinating or dreaming, or perhaps he is as John Pollock nicely illustrates, simply a brain being kept alive in the lab of a scientist, continually being fed fictional experiences.[87] The foundationalist is committed to taking all of these possibilities seriously. So, the point is clear: one can never have enough justification of an external empirical belief to guarantee the truth of that belief (and this is precisely what is required for hard justification.) So hard justification also fails, and it appears that as it goes, so goes epistemic foundationalism.

SECTION 1.10: OBJECTIONS TO COHERENTISM

In Section 1.3, I followed Moser in enumerating three traditional types of coherence theories of justification. These are (i) coherence as logical consistency, (ii) coherence as logical implication, and (iii) coherence as explanation. The first, coherence as logical consistency (i), offers that two beliefs are in a coherence relation and are therefore, justified just in case it is logically possible for both beliefs to be true. Coherence as logical implication (ii) offers that two beliefs cohere if and only if the truth of one logically guarantees the truth of the other. The third sort of theory, coherence as explanation (iii) offers that two beliefs are in a coherence relation just in case one belief explains the truth value of the other.

I will consider this first sort first, but only briefly. The second two types of coherence theories are often confused and the third (the strongest theory) entails the second. Therefore, I will concentrate my attack on the general principles of types (ii) and (iii) coherence.

The weakest of the three types of theories (in terms of justification) is (i) coherence as logical consistency. The notion that any two beliefs are justified if it is logically possible

---

87   John Pollock, Contemporary Theories of Knowledge, 1986.

that they are both true is untenable. Let me illustrate. The following two beliefs are both logically possible: *Smith owns a Chevy* and *Jones is in London.* However, would we really consider these two statements, or perhaps more accurately, this system of statements to be justified without any further evidence? The fact that they are both logically possible (i.e. logically consistent) is irrelevant. Let's look closer: If we call the first statement about Smith *s* and the second statement about Jones *t*, we will notice something epistemically disturbing. The system of beliefs {s, t} is logically consistent, and thus, justified. However, the system {s, not-t} is also logically consistent, and thus, justified. It seems quite strange that a statement and its negation can both be justified relative to the same coherent system at the same time. While logical consistency may indeed be necessary for justification, it is hardly sufficient. Bonjour, a coherentist, recognizes this, writing, "Coherence is not to be equated with consistency. A coherent system must be consistent, but a consistent system need not be very coherent."[88]

So, we are left with coherence as logical implication and/or as explanation. As I stated above, these two types of theories are very similar, often coextensive, and confused by some philosophers. For the remainder of this section, I will concern myself with the general principles of types (ii) and (iii) coherence theories, or what I will call, the *general theory of coherence.* By this, I mean simply "the view that the epistemic warrant . . . of empirical statements derives *entirely* from coherence and not at all from any sort of foundation"[89] and that while justification is wholly inferential, it "circles

---

[88]   Bonjour, 1976, p. 122.

[89]   ibid. 116.

back on itself,"[90] forming a circle or web or otherwise closed system in which the "primary unit of epistemic justification is such a system"[91] of logically and empirically connected beliefs.

I see five important criticisms to coherence theory. Some of these are articulated by Bonjour, who ultimately defends a coherentist view. I will consider each of these in turn. It is my hope to show that coherentism is insufficient as a theory of justification.

(1.) The most obvious and also the most popular objection to coherence theories of epistemic justification is what I will call the *problem of circularity*. The problem is this: Coherentist justification begs the question. The paradigm of justification advocated by coherence theorists relies on premise beliefs supporting justificandum beliefs which in turn are called on to support the original premise beliefs. To put it another way, coherence "depends on *its own* logically prior justification: It cannot be justified unless it is *already* justified."[92]

Coherence theorists might respond in one of two conceivable ways: (i) He might retort that the so-called *begging the question fallacy* itself begs the question by assuming that justification must be linear in nature. Or (ii) he might suggest, as Bonjour has, that there are two levels of justification questions – particular and global – and that it is illegitimate to ask for justification on only one or the other. But both of these rejoinders merely stave off the objection; they do not answer it.

(2.) A second criticism concerns the origins of the beliefs

---

in the coherent system. According to the basic axioms of the theory, individual beliefs can be evaluated for justification only one at a time and only in relation to the rest of the system. Therefore, for a belief to be justified (or even to be tested for justification) there must already be other beliefs in the system. But where did these primordial beliefs come from? How did they originally become part of the system? And how were they justified? Many coherentists have evaded this question or dismissed it as unimportant[93] but it seems to me that this question is very important. Contextualists like Wittgenstein have been concerned with the nature and origins of our first beliefs, and it seems deeply relevant whether these beliefs are an "inherited background"[94] into which we are born as Wittgenstein has claimed, or if they are empirically foundational, or if they have come into existence in some other way. Bonjour's response is that these first beliefs are accepted because they are *empirically introspective beliefs* which could hardly be wrong.[95] But, as I will show in the third objection, this must involve an appeal to non-coherence justification. The mysterious nature of these first beliefs and the web itself show coherentism to be problematic.

(3.) A third (and related) objection to the general coherence theory is that it cannot allow for input from the world. According to the coherence theory, all justification is inferential in nature. But observational statements which constitute new sense data are surely not inferential. Therefore, the web of beliefs cannot allow any new empirical information into it.

---

[93]   Bonjour, 1976, pp. 135-9.

[94]   Wittgenstein, 1969. §94.

[95]   Bonjour, 1976, p. 130-2.

This has been for most coherence theorists a particularly obdurate objection. Bonjour, however, has recently developed a uniquely sophisticated brand of coherentism that seems *prima facie* to be able to allow such new information. He alleges that there is a key misunderstanding being made. The distinction between a belief being *arrived at* inferentially and a belief being *justified* inferentially is being overlooked. Moreover, it may well be (and Bonjour says it should be) that one of the beliefs in our system is that *certain types of observational statements in certain situations are highly likely to be true.*[96]

But why should this be a belief in our system? How did it come to be in our system? There seems to be three ways that such a belief could be part of the coherent system: (a) the belief is a 'given' – it is assumed that such a belief will always be a founding member in such a system. This possibility seems wrong, for this would imply that there were empirically foundational and non-inferentially justified beliefs, or alternately, contextually basic beliefs, both of which are inconsistent with coherentism, by the coherence theorist's own admission. (b) The belief could be a new empirical belief.[97] This is problematic because it is by this belief's previous membership in the system that we can be justified that new empirical beliefs can enter the system. This would be a new circularity problem, and one that appears even more vicious than the original. (c) The belief could arise from within the system after one has enough experience to see that the belief is coherent. But no coherentists that I am aware of have taken this position and I cannot imagine how an argument for such a position might go. In any case, it

---

[96]   ibid. Section III.
[97]   see Bonjour, 1976, Part III.

assumes that there are already coherent beliefs in the system, which brings us back to the second objection.

(4.) Fourth (and also related), all revisions within the system involve a choice as to which beliefs to retain and which ones to discard. But how could we possibly methodically (non-arbitrarily) choose which beliefs to retain? Of course, the simple answer is that we retain those beliefs which are coherent with our system, but what if we have a number of new empirical beliefs which are incoherent with the system? Bonjour retorts that in such cases we side with our direct *observational beliefs*.[98] (If we didn't do this, we could hardly revise our system in any significant and meaningful way.) But why should this be so? What is our justification for claiming this to be so? Why should direct observational beliefs take precedence over our other beliefs? The only answer that I can see is that observational beliefs possess a degree of epistemic warrant independent of coherence, but Bonjour and other coherentists have emphatically denied this and clearly this notion is inconsistent with the general coherence theory, which holds that *all* epistemic warrant is inferential and comes from the coherent system.

(5.) Perhaps the strongest and most important objection to the general coherence theory of justification is that there are many examples of independently coherent systems which are inconsistent with each other. In these situations, coherentism is not able to satisfactorily answer how these rival systems could come into being, how one coherent system could altogether replace another coherent system, or why one coherent system should be preferred over another coherent system. Let me illustrate: In Euclidean geometry, space is thought to be a flat plane on which two parallel lines

---

[98] ibid. 136.

can continue forever without meeting. In post-Euclidean geometry, however, it is accepted that space is *curved* and that parallel lines *do* eventually meet. These two views are independently coherent, yet they are mutually inconsistent. They cannot both be true. Moreover, both seem to be descriptive of reality (from some perspective or another.) How do we account for two independently coherent, yet mutually inconsistent systems and how can one whole system replace a rival system?

There are many examples of mathematical and theoretical systems which are independently coherent yet mutually inconsistent. There are even completely coherent alternative maths which begin with axioms such as 2+2=5. But these are rational systems. What about systems of empirical beliefs? In the 13th century, it was commonly held that the Earth was the center of the universe and that the sun traveled around it. These were axioms in a coherent web of beliefs. There were many other accepted beliefs with which these axioms were coherent. They were coherent with religious doctrine, human pride, Ockham's razor, most of the scientific data of the day, and common experience (it sure looks like the sun is traveling around us — who in the 13th century would have imagined that the Earth they were standing upon was rotating and moving at hundreds of miles per second?)

Additionally, the Copernican hypothesis is completely and radically inconsistent with the Ptolemeac view, and yet this Copernican model *has replaced* the geo-centric model. The general coherence theory cannot account for the birth of wholly original systems in societies that already subscribe to a coherent system. Nor can it explain how one independently coherent system can be replaced by another independently coherent system with which it is incompatible. Yet, this is precisely what occurred in the Copernican revolution. The coherence theory cannot tell us why one coherent system should be preferred over another.

These five objections show the general coherence theory of justification to be highly problematic if not completely untenable. Further, coherentists, like foundationalists, agree that truth and justification are distinct and yet both necessary for empirical knowledge. This means that coherentists like foundationalists are susceptible to the original objection that I constructed in Section 1.9. Let me elaborate: We might ask, what is the relationship between coherence, justification, and truth? Why is a coherent system justified? Why are these beliefs considered likely to be true? The coherence theory must pass a meta-justificational test if it is to be accepted. If the coherence theory cannot bridge the gaps between coherence and justification and justification and truth, then it lacks a meta-justification. And if truth remains epistemically independent from justification and knowledge is at minimum a true justified belief, then either truth in inaccessible or justification is unattainable, and knowledge cannot be had. Notice that while this objection applies to epistemic coherentism, epistemic pragmatists and contextualists are not susceptible. Pragmatists avoid the objection because they identify truth and justification. Therefore, a justified belief is a true belief and all justified beliefs are knowledge. Contextualists avoid the dilemma because they do not accept the traditional account of knowledge (that it is at minimum a true justified belief.) Rather, contextual knowledge is simply a belief which has the proper grounds of support relative to a language-game, an issue-context, or some other kind of justifying backdrop.

SECTION 1.11: THE PRACTICALITY OF THE EXISTENTIAL EPISTEMOLOGIES

I have already said that I believe the existential epistemologies – epistemic pragmatism and epistemic contextualism – to be in some way superior to the older, more traditional paradigms of foundationalism and coherentism. One reason is that the existential epistemologies are not subject to the original and classic objections laid out in Sections 1.8-1.10. But, it seems to me that the existential epistemologies are also more eminent, practical, and relevant. How so? For more than two centuries, philosophers have spun their wheels over many of the same epistemological questions. One of the most obdurate of these is the challenge of skepticism: Can we know anything for certain? As an epistemologist raised in the western tradition, I understand and respect the importance of this question. I think (although some pragmatists would disagree with me) that this is not an entirely worthless question. It may be considered very worthwhile and relevant within a certain conceptual framework.

Pragmatists and contextualists have not simply sneezed at this question. Rather, they have chosen to look beyond it. It is not that they deem it unimportant (necessarily), but pragmatists and contextualists are practical. They realize that the answer has eluded thinkers for these 2000 years and that the answer may elude us for many years still. So, we ask, what do we do in the meantime? Pragmatists and contextualists have *chosen* to keep on working, to accept a conditional answer in practice, not because it is warranted, but because it is necessary for living. Foundationalists and coherentists, on the other hand, remain mired in the bog of uncertainty. Instead of making a practical choice, they have opted to keep struggling with the same questions. In a way, I see this attempt as valiant, though not very prudent and not very practical. Some pragmatists and contextualists may be calling for an end to the theoretical projects of traditional philosophy. I am not. I wish only to look beyond them.

In this chapter, I have distinguished four leading paradigms of epistemic justification according to their response to the regress problem of inferential justification. I have broadly outlined the traditional paradigms – epistemic foundationalism and epistemic coherentism — which attempt to find justified true beliefs through classic, static, immutable, non-social, non-evolutionary models of reasoning which take ontology as its first philosophy. Next, I broadly painted a picture of epistemic pragmatism and epistemic contextualism, which I call the "existential epistemologies." These paradigms search for contingent or dynamic knowledge in a practical, social, *praxis*-oriented, holistic, organic, evolutionary manner and take as their revolutionary starting point, the first philosophy of the concrete experience of the human animal's lived situation. Among the contributions of this section is the building of a bridge between pragmatic thinkers such as James and Dewey, contextualist thinkers such as Wittgenstein, and existentialists such as Camus and Sartre. Not only do each of these figures think of their project as a kind of *humanism*, but they each also respond similarly to the challenge of skepticism.

Next, I attempted to show that the existential epistemologies are superior to the traditional paradigms. This involved recounting several seminal arguments against foundationalism and coherentism and formulating an original argument which works against the traditional paradigms but not against epistemic pragmatism or epistemic contextualism. Finally, I discussed why I believe the existential epistemologies are more eminent, practical and relevant, and worthy of more serious philosophical attention.

In the next chapter, I will paint in greater detail and richer color the existential epistemologies of pragmatism and contextualism and I will distinguish the two by virtue of three general features. In Chapter 3, I will use my distinction to codify many contemporary epistemologists who have been referred to as "neo-pragmatists."

CHAPTER TWO

I N THE FIRST chapter of this book, I distinguished four of the leading paradigms of epistemic justification – epistemic foundationalism, coherentism, pragmatism, and contextualism according to their unique responses to the regress problem of inferential justification. Next, I explicated each of these families of theories in turn, taking care to distinguish the "existential" theories, epistemic pragmatism and contextualism from the traditional paradigms of foundationalism and coherentism. I discussed the important affinities shared by the existential paradigms, including their singular first philosophy, which is anti-skeptical and begins with an individual's "lived experience." Next, I provided several objections to each of the traditional paradigms. Some of these were popular objections from other philosophers while others were original. And finally, I discussed why I believe pragmatism and contextualism to be more practical and more immanent than foundationalism and coherentism.

In this chapter, I wish to explore epistemic pragmatism and epistemic contextualism in greater depth, identifying three features central to each, and distinguishing these two theories. To begin this analysis of pragmatism and contextualism, it is necessary to have clear paradigm cases of each theory to be studied. In this book, I take the later work of Ludwig Wittgenstein (primarily *On Certainty* and *Philosophical Investigations* and to a lesser extent, *Culture and Value* and the *The Blue and Brown Books)* to be paradigmatic of epistemic contextualism, and I take the mature work of William James and John Dewey to represent the paradigm of epistemic pragmatism. Surprisingly little work has been done building bridges between Wittgenstein and William James and almost nothing has been written about the relationship of Wittgenstein and Dewey. I wish to begin this chapter by briefly discussing the existing scholarship that compares Wittgenstein with James.

SECTION 2.1: WITTGENSTEIN AND JAMES

"Because Wittgenstein and James are typically placed in two distinct traditions of contemporary philosophy, their relationship has not often been taken into account. Wittgenstein commentators tend not to have studied James, and students of James often know little about Wittgenstein."[99] Of course, Wittgenstein and James never met. Wittgenstein began his academic work at Cambridge (at first in engineering) a year after James' death in America. G. E. M. Anscombe, the foremost translator of Wittgenstein's work, said, "not only had Wittgenstein not read *Pragmatism,* . . . but if he *had* read it, he would have hated it."[100] The "received view" on the subject is that the only importance that James had for Wittgenstein is that Wittgenstein felt James had committed

---

[99]   Russell B. Goodman, Wittgenstein and William James. Cambridge, U.K.: Cambridge University Press, 2002. p. 5.

[100] ibid. Preface, ix.

some "fundamental errors in the philosophy of mind."[101] But according to thinkers like A. C. Jackson and Russell B. Goodman, James's work "exerted a vast *positive* influence on Wittgenstein's philosophy, early and late."[102] Jackson, a student of Wittgenstein's, reports that "Wittgenstein very frequently referred to James in his lectures, even making on one occasion – to everybody's astonishment – a precise reference to a page number!"[103] Goodman tells us that at "one point after his return to philosophy in the 1930s, James's *Principles of Psychology* was the only book of philosophy visible on Wittgenstein's bookshelves[,]"[104] and that in Wittgenstein's *Remarks on the Philosophy of Psychology, Vol. 1, . . .* James is mentioned more than any other person (nine times)."[105] Elsewhere, Goodman writes,

> James came to be the object of some of Wittgenstein's most deeply reaching criticisms, yet Wittgenstein loved and trusted him from the start. He read James's *Varieties of Religious Experience* in 1912, in his first year as a student of philosophy at Cambridge, when he wrote to Russell: "Whenever I have time now I read James's *Varieties of Religious Experience*. This book does me a *lot* of good."[106]

---

[101] ibid. Preface, viii.

[102] ibid. Preface, viii.

[103] ibid. 10.

[104] ibid. 3.

[105] ibid. 10.

[106] ibid. 3.

In his 2002 book, *Wittgenstein and William James,* a cornerstone piece of scholarship in the rich, but largely untracked forest of James-Wittgenstein research, Goodman gives compelling evidence that James's work, not only on psychology and religion, but also on pragmatism was of great importance to Wittgenstein. In the Preface to this book, Goodman asserts that the "earliest commentator on Wittgenstein's relation to pragmatism is Wittgenstein himself."[107] In fact, in the notes that would posthumously become the book *On Certainty* as well as in his *Remarks on the Philosophy of Psychology,* Wittgenstein questions whether he himself, might not be a pragmatist. In the remainder of this chapter, I will explore this relationship between Wittgenstein and pragmatism, in the end, spotting three subtle but important points of distinction between the two.

SECTION 2.2: EPISTEMIC PRAGMATISM EXPLORED

The origin of the term 'pragmatism' is credited to C. S. Peirce, but I am not taking Peirce to be a paradigm of epistemic pragmatism in this book. Clearly, Peirce must in some way be considered a pragmatist. After all, he is the so-called father of the movement. But the sort of pragmatism that Peirce maintained is different in many ways from the mature epistemic, metaphysical, and humanistic view of James and Dewey. Peirce's pragmatism was essentially a theory of meaning. A young William James shared with Peirce the idea that many metaphysical dilemmas could be resolved by using a pragmatic principle to determine the meaning of equivocated or otherwise confused concepts. When, in his

[107]   ibid. Preface, ix.

essay, "Humanism and Truth," James applied the pragmatic principle to the term, 'truth', pragmatism grew into a theory of truth as well as of meaning. Throughout James's career, pragmatism became also a theory of knowledge and "of man."[108] Dewey further developed pragmatism into the all-encompassing worldview that it is today. In this section, I wish to explore epistemic pragmatism in greater depth, along the way clearing up some popular and obdurate misconceptions about pragmatism.

In Chapter One, we discovered that epistemic pragmatism is an "existential" epistemology, or as Putnam might say, it is an epistemology with a human face.[109] It emphasizes the primacy of practice or praxis. Pragmatism is an epistemology that recognizes the social, coherent, and contingent aspects of justification. It appreciates the importance of language and conceptual frameworks in the human animal's pursuit of knowledge. And it is an epistemology that rejects in total the traditional paradigms of foundationalism and coherentism. However, while this tells us much that is rare and interesting about epistemic pragmatism, it will not serve as a definition for all of these characteristics are true of epistemic contextualism as well.

Patrick Dooley writes, "James suggests that pragmatism involves a new orientation in that it conceives philosophy to be a practical, concrete, problem-solving enterprise."[110] In his book, *Meaning and Action: A Critical History of Pragmatism,* H. S. Thayer contrasts epistemic pragmatism

---

[108] Patrick Kiaran Dooley, Pragmatism as Humanism: The Philosophy of William James. Chicago: Nelson-Hall, 1974. p. 115.

[109] Hilary Putnam, Realism with a Human Face, 1990.

[110] Dooley, p. 118.

with the "spectator theory of knowing" in which minds passively receive and reflect upon "the show of things going on."[111] "Pragmatism — on the other hand, and this is a thesis of some force . . ." Thayer continues, "emphasizes the practical character of reason and reality."[112] Does this mean that pragmatists must only ask practical questions like where is our next meal coming from and avoid all philosophical ones? Some pundits (even some pragmatists) seem to think so, but this is not the case according to James. There is much beyond food and shelter that is of practical importance to human beings. Thayer writes, "Pragmatism is not to be condemned for holding that only 'practical thinking' about food, shelter, family, and business affairs is 'real[:]'"[113]

> In his Berkeley lecture, James examines the metaphysical option – materialism or theism. He first poses the hypothetical case of deciding this option in the last moment of time in the universe. In this instance since there is no possibility of future conceivable effects, there is no pragmatic difference between believing the world to be matter or a creation of God: 'Thus if no *future* detail of experience or conduct is to be deduced from our hypothesis, the debate between materialism and theism becomes quite idle and insignificant.' However, if we take the world as it is, with a future before

---

[111]   H. S. Thayer, Meaning and Action: A Critical History of Pragmatism. Indianapolis: Bobbs-Merrill Company, 1968. p. 425.

[112]   ibid. 425.

[113]   ibid. 425.

it, the theism/materialism option becomes meaningful.[114]

Thus, one salient aspect of the practical character of reality that pragmatists must consider is the possibilities of the future. Thayer writes, "Insofar as knowledge and action can be addressed to future possibilities, *possibility* is in some sense a trait of reality."[115] In "The Development of American Pragmatism," Dewey writes, "The doctrine of the value of consequences leads us to take the future into consideration. And this taking into consideration of the future takes us to the conception of the universe whose evolution is not finished, of a universe which is still in James' term 'in the making' . . .."[116] In *Pragmatism,* James writes, "What conceivable effects of a practical kind the object may involve – what sensations we are to expect from it and what reactions we must prepare. Our conception of these effects, whether immediate or remote, is then for us the whole of our conception of the object."[117] Finally, Patrick Dooley writes, "This instrumental view of knowledge holds that the meaning of an idea is not established by reducing it to the sense impressions from which it was derived; rather, meanings are to be located in the *consequences* of an idea or belief."[118]

Furthermore, epistemic pragmatism is a humanistic, existential theory of justification which concentrates on *specific* problems of knowledge. The bulk of the history of epistemology has been a struggle for epistemic knowledge

---

[114] Dooley, p. 120.

[115] Thayer, p. 426.

[116] Dewey, "Development of American Pragmatism" p. 25.

[117] James, Pragmatism, 43.

[118] Dooley, 119.

in general. But pragmatists have reconsidered this goal and shifted the epistemic paradigm. James writes, "the effective meaning of any philosophical proposition can always be brought down to some *particular* consequence in our future practical experience, whether active or passive; the point lying rather in that fact that the experience must be particular, than in the fact that it must be active."[119] Dewey writes, "there is no problem of knowledge in general."[120] However, there are, "[i]n ordinary life . . . problems a-plenty of knowledge in particular[.]"[121] And it is these epistemic problems that pragmatists choose to focus on. James's pragmatic principle asks us to take a *specific* belief and ask what practical consequences come from it. The consequences of a specific belief's veracity determine its truth. "The true is only the expedient in the way of our thinking. . .."[122] This is perhaps the most often misunderstood element of pragmatist epistemology. Even Bertrand Russell argues that pragmatism is absurd on the grounds that whatever has good results, or makes me happy is what is true.[123] Putnam writes,

> As his critics read this, what James is saying
> is that if the consequences of believing that
> *p* are good for humanity, then *p* is true. It
> is thus that Russell can write, "I find great

---

[119]   James, Collected Essays and Reviews, 412.

[120]   John Dewey, "The Need for a Recovery of Philosophy," 1917. The Essential Dewey, Volume 1: Pragmatism, Education, and Democracy. Edited by Hickman and Alexander. Bloomington: Indiana University Press, 1998. p. 56.

[121]   ibid. 56.

[122]   Hilary Putnam, Pragmatism: An Open Question, 1995. p. 8.

[123]   see Bertrand Russell, Philosophical Essays, 1966. pp. 116-125.

> intellectual difficulties in this doctrine. It assumes that a belief is 'true' when its effects are good."[124]

Unfortunately, Russell's mischaracterization of James and Dewey's pragmatic doctrine has taken hold popularly. In his 2001 article, "Truth and Use," Hans Seigfried writes,

> The pragmatic reconstruction of the truth value of propositions as use value has been criticized for a long time, most notoriously by Bertrand Russell in the debate with John Dewey that followed the 1938 publication of the latter's *Logic: A Theory of Inquiry*. Judging from the present debate in textbooks, the pragmatic view is obviously untenable simply because true propositions are not necessarily useful and useful propositions are not always true.[125]

But of course, this is a gross mischaracterization and Putnam clarifies: ". . . the view often attributed to James – that a statement is true if it will make him *happy* to believe it – is explicitly *rejected* by him."[126] Hans Seigfried continues, "[Russell's] objection illustrates well what Dewey deplores as a common procedure in philosophical controversy, namely, "representation of the position of an opponent in the terms it would have if the critic held it; that is, the meaning it has not in its own terms but after translation

---

[124]   Putnam, Pragmatism: An Open Question, 1995. p. 8.

[125]   Hans Seigfried, "Truth and Use." Synthese 128. 2001. p. 1.

[126]   ibid. 9.

into the terms of an opposed theory."[127] In "Pragmatism and Radical Empiricism," James clarified what he means. The expedient, the useful are *"those ideas that we can assimilate, validate, corroborate, and verify. False ideas are those that we cannot."*[128] Thus, in "Pragmatism's Conception of Truth," James can conclude, "You can say of [a true belief] either that 'it is useful because it is true' or that 'it is true because it is useful.'"[129] The two come out to the same thing. (I will expand on this point in Section 2.4.)

Another misconception concerning epistemic pragmatism is that it is simply another version of traditional empiricism. This has been a stalwart misconception thanks to some of James's own statements. He acknowledges Aristotle, Locke, Berkeley, and Hume as his predecessors and subtitles one of his volumes, "A New Name for Some Old Ways of Thinking."[130] Here, he seems to be referring to empiricism. *Prima facie,* James's epistemology bares resemblance to traditional empiricism when he writes, "if it can make no practical difference whether a given statement be true or false, then the statement has not real meaning."[131]

> James begins his Lowell lectures with a discussion of the two prevailing tendencies in philosophy. He characterizes them as follows: "tender-minded" (rationalist, i.e. going

---

[127] Hans Seigfried, p. 1. Seifried goes onto to call this "the fallacy of inadvertent submission."

[128] James, "Pragmatism and Radical Empiricism," 1907. p. 311.

[129] James, "Pragmatism's Conception of Truth," 1907. Pragmatism: The Classic Writings. Edited by Thayer. Indianapolis: Hackett, 1982. p. 230.

[130] Dooley, 118.

[131] James, The Meaning of Truth. p.52.

> by principles, intellectualistic, idealistic,
> monistic, religious, free-willistic, dogmatical)
> and "tough-minded" (empiricist, i.e. going
> by facts, sensationalistic, materialistic,
> pluralistic, irreligious, fatalistic, skeptical).
> He then proposes that pragmatism is a *media
> via* between these two tendencies.[132]

James's "experiential, fact-based" epistemology "differs from traditional empiricism in that it embodies an instrumental view of mind which holds that the function of thought is to guide future actions."[133]

Section 2.3: Epistemic Pragmatism Defined

So, epistemic pragmatism is a social, coherent, contingent, existential theory of knowledge which emphasizes the practical by focusing on future possibilities and on specific, particular beliefs rather than on knowledge in general. It resembles traditional empiricism in some ways, but differentiates itself from earlier empirical theories of knowledge by its unique claim that the consequences of a belief determine its meaning and veracity. But still we have not defined epistemic pragmatism. And as I recorded earlier in this book, pragmatism by its very nature eludes easy classification and categorization. It may be improper or even impossible to define pragmatism, as the analytics so often try to define a term, by enumerating its necessary and sufficient conditions. In my 2002 article, "Who's a Pragmatist? Distinguishing Epistemic Pragmatism and

---

[132]   Dooley, 120.
[133]   ibid. 121.

Contextualism," which was a key impetus for this book, I attempted to give just such a definition according to three analytic criteria. Although I now view this enterprise as somewhat misguided, my attempt to formally define pragmatism, gave me new insight into the nature of pragmatism and hopefully, that work shed light on some important features common to pragmatists. I will begin this section by presenting the 'formal definition' of pragmatism as it was given in my 2002 paper. Then, I will explain why this attempted definition falls short. And finally, I will give a refined elucidation of what I think this radical and unique theory of knowledge is all about.

The first seemingly essential feature of epistemic pragmatism that I presented in my 2002 work is its unusual response to the regress problem of inferential justification. The reader will remember that this problem involves the apparent infinite regress of the chain of inferentially justified beliefs. Foundationalists argue that this regress terminates in empirically basic or non-inferentially justified beliefs, while coherentists hold that inferential justification is not linear, but instead circular and that the chain of beliefs closes in on itself to form a coherent web. Pragmatism's novel solution, and the first of the three representative features of epistemic pragmatism is (1) that *the regress problem is completely averted because beliefs are immediately justified or unjustified based upon the practical difference their veracity would make in our experience of and interaction with the world.*[134] Dewey writes,

---

[134] This is James view and Dewey seems to concur with it. See John Dewey, "The Development of American Pragmatism," p. 7.

> To avoid this regress, [the foundationalists] stop short and assert that this or that object or truth is directly known, by sense intuition, by rational intuition, as a direct deliverance of consciousness, or in some other way. But what is such a procedure except the essence of what Bentham called *ipse dixitism?* What is it but arbitrary dogmatism? Who guards the guardians? The theory which places knowledge in rounded out conclusions [pragmatism] is in no such dilemma. It admits the hypothetical status of all data and premises and appeals for justification to operations capable, when they are repeated, of yielding like results. The antecedents do not have to be substantiated by being carried back to earlier antecedents and so on; they are good and sound if they do what is wanted of them: if they lead to an observable result which satisfies the conditions set by the nature of the problem in hand.[135]

This is the pragmatist's response to the regress problem, and this is where epistemic pragmatism initially sets itself apart from all other paradigms of justification (including, as we shall see, epistemic contextualism.)

The unusual manner in which the pragmatist meets the regress problem is interesting and important, but it is only

---

[135]   John Dewey, The Quest for Certainty, 1929; The Later Works, Volume 4: 1925-1953, 1988. pp. 146-147. This position is echoed in James', "What Pragmatism Means," 1907. The Writings of William James, 1967. pp. 377-379.

the first of three features of epistemic pragmatism which I pointed to as essential in my earlier work. In addition to (1) *the regress problem is averted because beliefs are immediately justified or unjustified based upon the practical difference their veracity would make in our experience of and interaction with the world,* epistemic pragmatists and no other kind of theorists, I then maintained, must hold the following two (even more crucial) claims: (2) *There is no distinction between truth and justification*[136] *(or alternately, truth is defined in terms of justification or the processes of justification;)* and (3) *There is no distinction between the world (external to minds) and the world as we perceive and interact with it.* Taken together, I took (1), (2), and (3) to be the necessary and sufficient conditions for epistemic pragmatism; that is to say, taken together, (1), (2), and (3) constituted my analytic definition of epistemic pragmatism.

That these further principles, (2) and (3), are central to epistemic pragmatism was not simply my assertion, but a proposition that I felt was evidenced in the writings of Dewey, James, Rorty, and Putnam.[137] As for (2) that truth and justification are indistinct, James writes, "Truth for us

---

136   In this book, I am assuming a general and traditional definition of the term 'justification.' I mean of course, epistemic justification, not moral or religious. A justified belief is one that is likely to be true, but is not necessarily coreferential with truth. That is, I am not assuming that if a belief is justified it is necessarily true, nor that if it if true it is necessarily justified.

137   One might ask how I can rely on quotations and textual references from contemporary philosophers like Rorty and Putnam, whose status as "pragmatists" has yet to be dealt with, to define pragmatism. I believe I am free from contradiction here because I consult these thinkers here only

is simply a collective name for verification processes . . ."[138] Dewey agrees with James that "any philosopher who applies this empirical method, without the least prejudice in favor of pragmatic doctrine, can be led to conclude that 'truth' means verification, or if one prefers, that verification either actual or possible, is the definition of truth."[139] Rorty writes, "Pragmatists think that if it makes no difference to practice, it should make no difference to philosophy. This conviction makes them suspicious of the distinction between justification and truth, for that difference makes no difference to my decisions about what to do."[140] He further writes, "To . . . [the classical pragmatists,] the difference between true beliefs considered as useful nonrepresentational mental states, and as accurate (and *therefore* useful) representations of reality, seemed a difference that could make no difference to practice. No one profits from insisting on the distinction, [they] concluded, except for those who enjoy entertaining make-believe doubts."[141] Finally, Putnam concurs, saying

---

as specialists about pragmatism. I am not assuming that their views are paradigmatic of epistemic pragmatism.

[138] James, "Pragmatism's Conception of Truth," 1907. The Writings of William James, 1977. p. 236.

[139] Dewey, "The Development of American Pragmatism," p. 7.

[140] Richard Rorty, "Is Truth a Goal of Inquiry? Donald Davidson versus Crispin Wright," 1995. Truth and Progress, 1998. p. 19.

[141] ibid. 20. Rorty takes many of the continental philosophers to be agreeing with the pragmatists on this point. I have chosen not to include a discussion about continental philosophy in this paper. Although such a discussion might be deserved, I will limit myself to asserting the following in this paper. If some continental philosopher agrees with principles (1), (2), and (3) above, then they should be considered an epistemic pragmatist. (This is not to say that if they agree with all three,

that pragmatists redefine truth "as the meeting of tests for truth."[142] Because it makes no practical difference to my actions or attitudes whether a belief is true or is merely accepted as true, and since a belief that is accepted as true is a justified belief, the pragmatist believes there is no practical reason to distinguish truth from justification. And if there is no practical reason for a distinction, then, the pragmatist reasons, there is no distinction.

In support of (3) that pragmatists hold that appearance and reality are indistinct, Dewey writes, "things . . . are what they are experienced as."[143] James writes, "The doctrine of pragmatism has in it the assumption of *radical empiricism: the notion that everything . . . is experienceable.*"[144] Rorty writes, ". . . we have learned (from Nietzsche and James, among others) to be suspicious of the appearance-reality distinction."[145] Putnam agrees, saying that a central tenet of pragmatism is ". . . the doctrine that perception is (normally)

---

then they are a pragmatist in general. As I said early in this section, there is much more to pragmatism than its epistemic part. Therefore, it is possible that one could agree with all the tenets of epistemic pragmatism without being a pragmatist in general.) If they do not agree with all three, they should not be called an epistemic pragmatist.

142 Putnam, Pragmatism: An Open Question. 1995. p. 2.

143 Dewey, "The Postulate of Immediate Empiricism," 1905. The Essential Dewey, Volume 1: Pragmatism, Education, and Democracy, 1998. p. 115.

144 James, "Pragmatism and Radical Empiricism," 1907. The Writings of William James, 1977. p. 314.

145 Rorty, introduction to Truth and Progress, 1998. p. 1. Again, if Nietzsche holds this view, it does not follow that he is a pragmatist in general; see footnote 20.

of objects and events 'out there', and not of private sense data."[146]

Let me summarize then my once-held definition of epistemic pragmatism: pragmatism (1) *avoids the regress problem of inferential justification by arguing that our beliefs are immediately justified or unjustified based on the practical difference their veracity would make in life.* Additionally, pragmatists claim (2) *that there is no distinction between truth and justification (or that truth is defined in justificatory terms.)* And finally they hold (3), *that there is no distinction between the world and the world as we perceive and interact with it.*

SECTION 2.4: THE PRAGMATISTS ON "KNOWLEDGE"

I do not disavow the work I did for my 2002 article. I believe that work made a contribution to epistemology and I believe I brought some much due attention to the existential theories of knowledge. I still believe my elucidation of pragmatism and contextualism in that work to be more correct than not. But I hope that through critiquing that article now, I can shed more light on epistemic pragmatism and contextualism and present a more accurate view of each. The first and most trenchant mistake I made in 2002 was to assume that pragmatism could be captured by an essentialist project. Perhaps with my Platonic and analytic rearing in philosophy, this mistake was inevitable, but I now believe it is most important to recognize that pragmatism does not easily succumb to an analytic definition. If we do not see this, we will miss entirely the radical and revolutionary message

---

[146]   Putnam, Pragmatism: An Open Question. 1995. p. 7.

that James and Dewey were trying to convey. If pragmatism is essentially anything, it is essentially anti-essentialist. The epistemological method of the early pragmatists was experimental, fallible, and human. Moreover, pragmatism is a holistic theory, and so it is a somewhat misbegotten idea to study the epistemological without the metaphysical, the metaphysical without the ethical, the ethical without the aesthetic, and so forth. James quite deliberately conflates such terms as "knowledge," "truth," and "good." In every metaphysical investigation, there is an investigation of knowledge and ways of knowing. In every epistemological investigation, we make value judgments.

A related failure of the 2002 paper was an incomplete discussion of what it means for pragmatists to identify truth with justification, appearance with reality. I do not wish to retract this part of my definition, only to present a fuller and clearer picture of what this means. Not every pragmatist is an anti-realist. At least, not every pragmatist claims to be. Some pragmatists, it seems, would *prima facie* reject for instance that appearance is to be equated with reality. To explain why I continue to maintain my view against reputable opposition, I must discuss in more depth the pragmatist notions of "truth" and "knowledge."

What does James mean when he writes that truth is to be defined in terms of verification? He means quite simply that these two enterprises cannot be partitioned. When we are looking for truth, we are at the same time asking *how do we know what is true*? When we are looking for what is real, we must ask at the same time, *what do my experiences tell me is real?* In his "Essays in Radical Empiricism," James writes,

> Nothing shall be admitted as fact except what can be experienced at some definite

> time by some experient; and for every
> feature of fact ever so experienced, a definite
> place must be found somewhere in the final
> system of reality. In other words, everything
> real must be experienceable somewhere,
> and every kind of thing experienced must
> somewhere be real.[147]

But surely James and Dewey aren't denying the existence of hallucinations or mirages, or other optical illusions. In these cases, surely, appearance and reality don't match up. *Prima facie,* the pragmatists's position seems counter-intuitive, for example, when Dewey writes, "Even dreams, hallucinations, etc. . . . are not something outside of the regular course of events . . .. They are not cognitive distortions of real things; they are *more* real things."[148] But of course, Dewey is not saying that the bedsheet fluttering in the night breeze really is a ghost. The problem here seems to be that we are presuming a correspondence theory of truth. (I will address this point in fuller detail momentarily.) According to the pragmatists, truth is matter of leading. And dreams and hallucinations are things which may lead. In "The Need for a Recovery in Philosophy," Dewey writes, "Dreams have often been taken as prognostics of what is to happen; they have modified conduct. A hallucination may lead a man to consult a doctor; such a consequence is right and proper."[149] Dooley writes that for James, "The relations between our ideas and matters of fact are obviously mutable

---

[147] James, "Essays in Radical Empiricism," p. 160.

[148] Dewey, "The Need for a Recovery of Philosophy," 1917. The Essential Dewey, Volume 1: Pragmatism, Education, and Democracy, 1998. p. 56.

[149] ibid. 58.

and dependent upon our temporary purposes[,]"[150] and "the world, as it is experienced, presents no duality; reality is pure neutral experience."[151] Since it makes no practical difference to my actions or attitudes whether the world really is like I perceive it to be through my experiences in it, or not, there is likewise, no practical reason for making an appearance-reality distinction, and thus, the distinction is not made in pragmatism.

It is helpful again to remind ourselves what James says about truth, that it is a matter of leading. What is true is what leads us to success. What is justified is what leads us to where we wish to go. In Chapter One of this book, I wrote that pragmatists respond in a certain way to the problem of skepticism – they respond in a way that leads them out of that jungle into the light of day. I wish to return to the problem of skepticism presently in order to illustrate more clearly how pragmatists have reconstructed the notion of 'knowledge.' In his 1874 article, "The Ethics of Belief,"[152] William Clifford tells us that believing without proper truth-conducive justification is "wrong always, everywhere, and for anyone."[153] To explain why he thinks unjustified belief is epistemically and morally wrong, Clifford tells us this story: A shipowner is about to send a ship full of immigrants to the new land. The shipowner is warned that the ship is old and weathered and not overly well built at the start, and

---

[150]   Dooley, p. 130.

[151]   ibid. 136.

[152]   William Clifford. "The Ethics of Belief," from Lectures and Essays, reprinted in Philosophy of Religion: Selected Readings. Edited by William L. Rowe and William J. Wainwright. Third Edition. Harcourt Brace College Publishers, 1998. pp. 456-461.

[153]   ibid. 460.

may not make the long journey. Although he could have the ship inspected and repaired if necessary, the shipowner decides to trust in Providence. "It has made many voyages," he reasons. "Surely, it will make this one also." Ultimately, the ship sinks and the immigrants all perish. We can see why Clifford feels that this unjustified belief is unwise. It can lead to disastrous consequences. But what if the ship had made it to the new land successfully? In that case too, says Clifford, the shipowner would be guilty, "because he had no right to believe on such evidence as was before him."[154] What makes holding a belief correct or incorrect is not, for Clifford, simply a matter of whether that belief is true or false, or even whether it is fruitful or unfruitful, but rather, of how it originated. The danger of faith is not only that we might have a false belief or even that we should pass on a false belief to others, although this is bad enough. Still worse, if we should be in the habit of not seeking truth-conducive evidence for our beliefs, we may become credulous and savage. Analytic philosophers have maintained such a view historically and we can easily see why. But part of the revolution of the early pragmatists is their questioning of this view, and their claim that there are other reasons that count as justification besides *truth-conducive reasons*. I will call any reason that tends to show that a belief is true according to the correspondence theory of truth a truth-conducive reason and I will call a reason that tends to show that a belief may be useful or well-leading a *pragmatic reason*. James, I believe, successfully argues that pragmatic reasons are enough to pass for justification in some circumstances and hence, to pass as truth. James argues that reliance on pragmatic reasons can be not only morally and epistemically permissible, but it can

---

[154] ibid. 456.

sometimes even be salvific or hero-making. James discusses the importance of hero-making faith in "Ethical Importance of the Phenomenon of Effort," writing,

> The world thus finds in the heroic man its worthy match and mate; and the effort which he is able to put forth to hold himself erect and keep his heart unshaken is the direct measure of his worth and function in the game of human life. He can *stand* this Universe. He can meet it and keep up his faith in it in presence of those same features which lay his weaker brethren low. He can still find a zest in it, not by "ostrich-like forgetfulness," but by pure inward willingness to face it with these deterrent objects there. And hereby he makes himself one of the masters and lords of life. He must be counted with henceforth; he forms a part of human destiny. Neither in the theoretic nor in the practical sphere do we care for, or go for help to, those who have no head for risks, or sense for living on the perilous edge. . . . But just as our courage is so often a reflex of another's courage, so our faith is apt to be a faith in someone else's faith. We draw new life from the heroic example.[155]

---

[155] William James. "Ethical Importance of the Phenomenon of Effort," The Writings of William James, Edited by John J. McDermott. Chicago: University of Chicago Press, 1967. p. 716.

Under what conditions are pragmatic reasons morally and epistemically acceptable? First, one can rely on pragmatic reasons only when the choice one must make is *intellectually undecidable.* If a little bit of thinking could decide the issue one way or the other then we cannot simply choose to have faith or to go with our pragmatic reasons. Also, the decision in question must constitute a *genuine option.* A genuine option is a choice which James defines as *living, forced,* and *momentous.* A living option is one where there exist at least two real possibilities to choose between. In addition, to being live, a genuine option must be forced. A forced option is one where a decision must be made, or where choosing not to decide amounts to choosing one way or the other. Finally, a genuine option must be momentous. That is, it must be important and unique. Deciding to go to the grocery store to buy paper towels is not momentous. Nothing very important hinges upon the decision and the decision could be made again at any time in the future. Some decisions, however, like the decision of whether or not to believe in the Christian God may be very important. If a decision is intellectually undecidable and a genuine option – that is, living, forced, and momentous, James tells us we are permitted (epistemically and morally; remember James purposely conflates knowledge, truth, and goodness) to go with our pragmatic reasons. We may *will* ourselves to believe. Remember, again, reader, the existentialist's absurd choice.

Although the primary focus of this book is not to defend a specific theory of pragmatism or contextualism, or even to advocate for either paradigm generally, I am compelled to briefly defend James's point concerning pragmatic reasoning and willing to believe.

It seems clear to me that some truths cannot be realized

without first choosing to believe them. In some cases, it seems we can even create true beliefs by the act of believing. Take the cliché story of a man confronted by dangerous criminals in a dark alley. Instead of running from the criminals or fighting them, this man appeals to the good in the criminals, treats them as if they were loving people. And by treating the criminals if they were loving despite a lack of evidence to this effect, the criminals are made loving. On a personal level, I have learned the value of pragmatic reasoning in the classroom. Before meeting a new class that I am to teach, I have no good evidence about whether my students will be good students or bad students. By "good" I here simply mean intellectually honest critical truth seekers who are enthusiastic about philosophy. In fact, one could argue that I have inductive or circumstantial evidence that at least some of my students will not be good as it seems that I always in the past have had some students that lack enthusiasm or honesty or are not committed to finding truth. Nevertheless, when I walk into a new class, I choose to believe that all of my students are good students and I treat them as such. Although I could be wrong, I believe that my decision to believe in the goodness of my students helps bring about the virtues of enthusiasm and honesty and commitment to truth in them. My reasons for believing in the goodness of my students is not "truth-conducive." That is, the reason I believe it is not that I have good evidence that it is true according to the correspondence theory of truth. Rather, I believe that there are pragmatic or existential reasons why one might be justified in believing something. For example, I believe in the goodness of my students because I think some good will come of it and no harm will be done. Dewey, a social progressive and a member of such important organizations as the NAACP, lacked truth-conducive evidence that racial equality was achievable in the near future. However, it was the willingness to believe in the possibility of an egalitarian society, by progressive thinkers like Dewey, which enabled that society to become a real possibility.

Before I move on, I wish to examine what pragmatists have to say about truth and about their general metaphysical commitments. Not all scholars agree that pragmatists are engaging in metaphysics at all. Richard Rorty writes, "to pragmatists . . . although there is obviously a lot to be said about justification of various sorts of beliefs, there may be little to say about truth."[156] And Rorty is not alone. Many pragmatists have developed deflationist theories of truth in order to say as little as possible about metaphysics. The most interesting and perhaps most important attack against a pragmatist metaphysics comes from Charlene Haddock Seigfried. In her 2001 article, "Pragmatists Metaphysics? Why Terminology Matters," she writes that "pragmatism itself is an original and creative alternative to metaphysical thinking . . .."[157] And later she discusses the "pragmatist's emphatic assertions that metaphysics was the problem, not the solution":

> The centuries-long philosophical efforts to develop a metaphysics was considered by them at least a distraction from the concrete concerns of everyday life and at most a tragic detour away from everything that gives value and meaning to life. Dewey was

---

[156] Rorty, 1995. p. 19.

[157] Charlene Haddock Seigfried, "Pragmatist Metaphysics? Why Terminology Matters," Transactions of the Charles S. Peirce Society. Winter 2001. Volume XXXVII, Number 1. p. 13.

most emphatic in placing this philosophical original sin at the very origins of philosophy in the work of Plato and Aristotle. The alternative he advocated is clear: 'that which may be pretentiously unreal when it is formulated in metaphysical distinctions becomes significant with the drama of the struggle of social beliefs and ideals.[158]

Seigfried takes on this subject most seriously in her article, "Ghosts Walking Underground: Dewey's Vanishing Metaphysics." Therein, Seigfried argues that Dewey avoids doing metaphysics, discouraged others against metaphysics, and was "struggling to develop a post-Darwinian alternative to metaphysics."[159]

I would now like to take up the issue of whether or not the classical pragmatists engaged in metaphysics. I have said previously that I believe that pragmatists maintain certain metaphysical commitments. Among these are the fact that since pragmatists equate truth and justification, the pragmatist is committed to the denial of a recognition-transcendent truth and since pragmatists refuse to distinguish appearance and reality, pragmatists are committed to the denial of recognition-transcendent reality. Do James and Dewey have metaphysical projects and do I disagree with the careful arguments of Charlene Haddock Seigfried? To answer these questions, we must first ask, what do we mean by metaphysics and what do we mean by recognition-transcendent truth and reality?

By metaphysics, many philosophers simply mean an

---

[158]   ibid. 13-14.

[159]   ibid. 1.

attempt to understand the world, to understand what things exist and what things are. It seems clear to me that James and Dewey, two figures as historically important to science and scientific methodology as to philosophy, asked these questions. But "metaphysics" took on a deeper meaning after Kant. And I believe this deeper meaning was not lost on the pragmatists. In fact, Hans Seigfried tells us that "the connections between Kant and Dewey are perhaps much closer than some of us are inclined to believe."[160]

Pragmatists like James and Dewey reject metaphysics as it transcends our human experiences. That is to say, pragmatists have given up the noumenal. In his article, "A Short Catechism Concerning Truth," Dewey writes

> It is interesting to note that the opponents of pragmatism have been forced by the exegencies of their hostility to resuscitate a doctrine supposedly dead: the doctrine of unexperienceable, unknowable, "Things in Themselves." And as if this were not enough, they identify Truth with relationship to this unknowable. Thereby in behalf of the notion of truth in general, they land in scepticism with reference to the possibility of any truth in particular. The pragmatist *is* bound to deny *such* transcendence.[161]

There is little accord among Kantians as to what is the final conclusion of Kant's philosophy of metaphyiscs.

---

160 Hans Seigfried, p. 9.
161 Dewey, "A Short Catechism Concerning Truth," The Influence of Darwin on Philosophy. By John Dewey. Bloomington: Indiana University Press, p. 156.

But Hans Seigfried for one believes that Kant's project was similar to Dewey's, that in fact, Dewey finishes what Kant began. He writes, the "experimentalist revolution" was "initiated by Kant and completed by Dewey."[162] And again: "Both believe that their adoption of the experimental method constitutes a genuine breakthrough, and a case can be made for the claim that the pragmatic revolution, which arguably culminates in Dewey's *Logic: The Theory of Inquiry*, concludes what Kant's critical efforts began."[163] So, are the pragmatists engaged in metaphysics? In a broad sense, I believe so. Pragmatists are committed to understanding the world, but their pursuit is of a phenomenal metaphysics by epistemologically experimental means. In a narrow sense, I believe not. They reject the noumenal, the transcendent metaphysics of the thing in itself:

> If we acknowledge, Dewey argues, that the knowing of experimentally controlled constitutive inquiry is "one kind of interaction which goes on within the world", then we will have to find ways for revising our received concepts of truth and knowledge that continue to frustrate successful inquiry in philosophy just as they did in the empirical sciences before [the] experimental breakthrough[.][164]

Do pragmatists maintain a recognition-transcendent truth and reality? I believe not. When James argues that

---

162 Hans Seigfried, p. 10.
163 ibid. 2.
164 ibid. 1.

truth is defined in terms of verification and when Dewey claims that what is real is what we experience, I believe they are each in their own way insisting that we seek only the phenomenal (the thing as it appears) and not the noumenal (the thing in itself.)

Is pragmatism an idealist or a realist enterprise? In this matter, I must agree with Charlene Haddock Seigfried who writes,

> [P]ragmatism has sometimes been categorized as a version of realism and sometimes as idealism. But the originality of pragmatism cannot be fully grasped without recognizing that it is neither, because its analysis of concrete human experience rejects the metaphysical assumptions on which the distinction is based.[165]

In this section, I have attempted to show how the classical pragmatists have reconstructed the traditional notions of truth and knowledge. I would like to close this section with a quotation from Hans Seigfried which I think summarizes well pragmatist epistemology:

> Inquiry . . . is the transformation of an uncertain, unsettled, disturbed existential situation by operations that actually modify

---

[165] Charlene Haddock Seigfried, "The Pragmatist Sieve of Concepts: Description Versus Interpretation." The Journal of Philosophy. Volume LXXXVII, No. 11. November 1990. p. 585.

existing conditions such that restoration of integration can be effected.[166]

Section 2.5: Epistemic Contextualism Explored

In my 2002 article, "Who's a Pragmatist? Distinguishing Epistemic Pragmatism and Contextualism," I held that (1) pragmatists *avoid the regress problem of inferential justification by arguing that our beliefs are immediately justified or unjustified based on the practical difference their veracity would make in life.* Additionally, I suggested that pragmatists claim (2) *that there is no distinction between truth and justification (or that truth is defined in justificatory terms.)* And finally they hold (3), *that there is no distinction between the world and the world as we perceive and interact with it.* Although I no longer wholeheartedly endorse this "essentialist definition" of epistemic pragmatism, I continue to believe these are three central tenets that pragmatists share. Of course, there are others and many of these traits are common to contextualists as well. Like pragmatism, contextualism is an existential approach to epistemology. Like pragmatism, contextualism takes seriously the primacy of practice, social justification, coherence, contingency, and the importance of language and conceptual frameworks. And like pragmatism, contextualism rejects the traditional paradigms of epistemic foundationalism and coherentism. But of course, my aim in this section is not to show the similarities of these two theories. This has already been done. Rather, I hope to point out the subtle but important

---

[166]   Hans Seigfried, p. 7.

differences that make contextualism an independent and original existential paradigm of justification.

To understand contextualism, it is necessary to understand the epistemology of the later Wittgenstein, the paradigm contextualist. Many believe that Wittgenstein's epistemology is a version of foundationalism or coherentism. Wittgenstein is characterized as a type of foundationalist, for example, by Michael Williams in his 1991 book *Unnatural Doubts*[167] and as an epistemic coherentist in many of the works of Crispin Wright, including "Facts and Certainty."[168] In this section, I hope to show that Wittgenstein is neither a foundationalist nor a coherentist, but rather that his epistemology is a theory *sui generis.*

It is manifest why some critics would think that Wittgenstein was a kind of foundationalist, for he writes, "To be sure there is justification, but justification comes to an end."[169] And: "Somewhere we must be finished with justification...."[170] Though these assertions certainly sound foundational, there is a very important difference between Wittgenstein's contextualism and epistemic foundationalism. While foundationalists view our most basic empirical beliefs as epistemically justified, contextualists, like Wittgenstein, do not. Rather, he writes, "The difficulty is to realize the

---

[167] Michael Williams refers to Wittgenstein as a "local foundationalist", Unnatural Doubts. Oxford: Balckwell, 1991.

[168] Crispin Wright, "Facts and Certainty," Henriette Hertz Philosophical Lecture for the British Academy, December 1985, published in Proceedings of the British Academy LXXI, pp. 429-72.

[169] On Certainty, §192.

[170] ibid. §212. These claims, likewise, show that he is not an infinitist. See also §110, §204, and §449.

groundlessness of our believing."[171] And: Our foundational beliefs lie "beyond being justified or unjustified...."[172] It must be admitted that Wittgenstein's picture does closely resemble foundationalism. In fact, one might say that the model is *logically foundational*, though not *epistemically* so. By this, I simply mean that there do seem to be multiple levels of beliefs[173], and that higher order beliefs can be inferred from lower order ones, but not that higher order beliefs are epistemically justified if they are deducible from basic beliefs. Wittgenstein writes, "If you do know that *here is one hand,* we'll grant you all the rest. When we say that such and such a proposition can't be proved, of course that does not mean that it can't be derived from other propositions; any proposition can be derived from other ones. But they may be no more certain than it is itself."[174]

Likewise, Wittgenstein's theory of knowledge resembles, and in fact, borrows from coherence theories: ". . . my convictions do form a system, a structure[,]"[175] he writes. "What stands fast does so, not because it is intrinsically obvious or convincing, it is rather held fast by what lies around it."[176] There are (at least) two salient points of distinction between Wittgenstein's contextualism and epistemic coherentism. Once again, while coherentists view their web of beliefs as justified, Wittgenstein does not. Second, although contextualism is not foundational in an epistemic sense — that is, contextually basic beliefs lack epistemic justification — the way in which it proposes to stop

---

[171]   ibid. §166.

[172]   ibid. §359; see also §94.

[173]   ibid. §192, §212.

[174]   ibid. §1.

[175]   ibid. §102.

[176]   ibid. §144; see also §141-142, §225.

the regress of inferential justification *is* foundational, not coherentist. Wittgenstein believes that there *is* a foundation, but "[a]t the foundation . . . lies belief that is not founded."[177]

What I have said already may be enough to demonstrate that Wittgenstein's epistemology is distinct from foundationalism and coherentism. However, it seems to me that there is an even greater difference that can be pointed out. To see it, we must carefully explore Wittgenstein's view of the foundations of knowledge. For Wittgenstein, foundational beliefs lie beyond being epistemologically supportable, such that to ask for their justification would be either absurd or unthinkable. He compares the foundations of knowledge to the rules of a game.[178] Consider, for example, a chess player questioning, *why should the knight be allowed to move three spaces?* The only appropriate answer to such a question is *that's just how the game is played.* The rules may well be arbitrary, but if you do not accept them, you are not really playing chess. These foundations, he continues, are not atomic, independent propositions, like those that Moore attempts to enumerate.[179] Rather, they form a coherent system. Wittgenstein writes, "When we first begin to *believe* anything, what we believe is not a single proposition, it is a whole system of propositions. (Light dawns gradually over the whole.)"[180] Again: "It is not single axioms that strike me as obvious, it is a system in which consequences and premises give one another *mutual* support."[181]

More commonly, he avoids talking about the

---

177   ibid. §253; see also §94, §192, §238, §449.

178   ibid. §95, §496.

179   ibid. §6.

180   ibid. §141.

181   ibid. §142; see also §144.

foundations of knowledge as mere *propositions* or *axioms* at all. Rather, he calls them the *bedrock of the language-game.* The language-game is the inherited framework of all of our shared linguistic actions and practices. The bedrock of the language-game is the most basic foundation upon which the language-game rests. Let me elaborate:

The bedrock of the language-game, like the language-game itself is intimately tied up with *linguistic actions* and *practices.* Wittgenstein asserts, "As if giving ground did not come to an end sometime. But the end is not an ungrounded presupposition: it is an ungrounded way of acting."[182] Or: "Giving grounds, however, justifying the evidence, comes to an end; — but the end is not certain propositions' striking us immediately as true, i.e. it is not a kind of *seeing* on our part; it is our *acting,* which lies at the bottom of the language-game."[183]

Also, while this bedrock includes traditionally foundational sorts of beliefs, for instance, beliefs about memories and sensations, it also includes certain methodologies, attitudes, and doubts.[184] In short, it is a whole way of thinking and living. Wittgenstein gives us a humorous example to show us what he means: "When a child learns language it learns at the same time [for example] what is to be investigated and what not."[185] Consider a man who is looking for a lost object: ". . . he opens the drawer and doesn't see it there; then he closes it again, waits, and opens it once more to see if perhaps it isn't there now, and keeps on like that." This person "has not learned to looked

[182] ibid. §110.
[183] ibid. §204.
[184] ibid. §238.
[185] ibid. §472.

for things. . ... He has not learned the game that we are trying to teach him."[186] Elsewhere he writes, "Perhaps I shall do a multiplication twice to make sure, or perhaps get someone else to work it over. But shall I work it over twenty times, or get twenty people to go over it? And is that some sort of negligence? Would the certainty really be greater for being checked twenty times?"[187] Wittgenstein does not say that this extremely high level of philosophical skepticism is *incorrect*. Nor, on the other hand, is it *correct*. The beliefs and practices of our foundations cannot accurately be called correct or incorrect because the bedrock of the language-game *is not, itself, normative*. Rather, it is the descriptive background against which we make normative judgments. Of the foundational practices of human beings, Wittgenstein writes, "By this I naturally do not want to say that men *should* behave like this, but only that they do behave like this."[188] Again: "You must bear in mind that the language-game is so to say something unpredictable. I mean: it is not based on grounds. It is not *reasonable (or unreasonable)*. It is there — like our life."[189] Finally: "I did not get my picture of the world by satisfying myself of its correctness; nor do I have it because I am satisfied of its correctness. No: it is the inherited background against which I distinguish between true and false."[190] Such radical skepticism as exhibited in the examples above is simply not descriptive of the foundations of our language-game,[191] and therefore, anyone entertaining such skepticism does not share in our language-game.

---

[186]   ibid. §315.

[187]   ibid. §77.

[188]   ibid. §284; see also §82.

[189]   ibid. §559; italics added.

[190]   ibid. §94.

[191]   ibid. §317.

Another important aspect of the bedrock (and the language-game itself) is that it is not freely chosen. Wittgenstein's contextualist epistemology should not be confused with *conventionalism,* the theory propounded by Duhem and others, that our linguistic and scientific practices are constrained by rules that we have freely adopted by general agreement. According to Wittgenstein, we do not *choose* or *agree to* the regulations of the language-game. We are inducted into the language-game as we are inducted into society.[192] Finally, even the very foundation of the language-game is not stagnant. It is ever-changing, and as it changes, methods change, doubts change; even our concepts and the meanings of our words change.[193]

So, the bedrock of the language-game is an ever-changing, unchosen, inherited, descriptive, coherent system of principles, linguistic actions and practices (including methodologies, attitudes, and doubts), which are neither justified nor unjustified, and which forms the foundation of all our ordinary empirical knowledge. The basic beliefs of this bedrock (beliefs like *I know my name*[194] or *this is my foot*[195]) are not accepted because of any support that we have for them. They are accepted because they are beliefs which are necessary for us to accept if we wish to live meaningful lives. Wittgenstein writes, "My *life* consists in my being content to accept many things." [196] Again: ". . . somewhere I must begin with non-doubting; and that is not, so to speak, hasty but excusable . . ."[197] Finally: ". . . somewhere I must begin

---

[192] "(But not as if we chose this game!)", §317.

[193] ibid. §63, 65, 256, 336.

[194] ibid. §577.

[195] ibid. §360.

[196] ibid. §344.

[197] ibid. §150.

with an assumption or a decision."[198] For Wittgenstein, the foundations of knowledge are not necessarily propositional. Further, they are not epistemic, but rather existential. This clearly sets his epistemology apart from the traditional paradigms of justification, foundationalism and coherentism, and shows it to be a theory of knowledge *sui generis.*

SECTION 2.6: WITTGENSTEIN ON "KNOWLEDGE"

The reduction of Wittgenstein's worldview to some kind of foundationalism or coherentism is not the only misconception regarding his epistemology. There is widespread misunderstanding about his theory of knowledge in part due to the confusing way in which he employs the term 'knowledge.' Although not all scholars agree, I believe Wittgenstein maintains two distinct accounts of *knowledge* simultaneously. In his famous book, *Wittgenstein on Rules and Private Language*[199], Saul Kripke offers a biperspectival account of Wittgenstein's philosophy of language as regards *meaning.* In this section, I would like to present a biperspectival account of Wittgenstein's epistemology as regards *knowledge.* Then I will consider objections to this reading and investigate whether or not such a theory can hold up under philosophical scrutiny.

It is my claim that Wittgenstein uses the term 'knowledge' in two ways in his posthumous book, *On Certainty.* Of course, the book, *On Certainty,* is simply a collection of notes that Wittgenstein wrote late in his

---

[198] ibid. §146.

[199] Saul Kripke, Wittgenstein on Rules and Private Language. Cambridge: Harvard, 1982.

lifetime – a collection of notes which he never intended to be published. Had he intended the publication of these notes, he might have taken care to distinguish, for the sake of the reader, these two accounts of knowledge. But since these notes were written only for Wittgenstein's private use, he probably didn't feel it was necessary to remind himself of the two uses of 'knowledge' he maintains. One type of knowledge that Wittgenstein discusses in *On Certainty* is traditional epistemic knowledge, the sort of knowledge that analytic philosophers, including his mentors, Moore and Russell, seek. Concerning the possibility of this type of knowledge, Wittgenstein is skeptical. But there is another type of knowledge which Wittgenstein discusses, what I will call *contextual knowledge*, about which he is anti-skeptical. I will begin by discussing contextual knowledge.

Wittgenstein discusses two sorts of contextual knowledge. I will call these *contextually basic knowledge* and *higher order knowledge.* Higher order beliefs are those that may be inferred or deduced from contextually basic beliefs. At this point, a critic might object that I am mistakenly invoking a foundationalist model of empirical knowledge, after distinguishing contextualism from foundationalism only moments ago. The picture I am presenting does closely resemble foundationalism. In fact, as I stated earlier, one might say that the model is logically foundational, though not epistemically so. By this, I simply mean that there are multiple levels of beliefs and that higher order beliefs can be inferred from lower order ones, but not that higher order beliefs are epistemically justified if they are deducible from contextually basic beliefs. Another critic might object that Wittgenstein endorses an epistemic holism in which all of our beliefs are on the same level. Certainly, there are holistic and even coherentist elements in Wittgenstein's epistemology. However, I believe this second critic is also ultimately mistaken. Wittgenstein explicitly claims that "proposition[s] can be derived from other ones,"[200] and that some beliefs are more basic than others.[201]

A contextually basic belief, then, is one that is part of the bedrock of our language-game. Wittgenstein calls such a proposition an "irreversible belief," and says that it is a claim of which "I am not ready to let anything count as a disproof."[202] Elsewhere: "I would refuse to entertain any argument that tried to show the opposite."[203] Wittgenstein's examples of contextually basic knowledge include the knowledge of one's own name[204], or the recognition of one's own foot.[205] Such beliefs *must* be accepted as knowledge, *not because they are justified, but because they are impossible to live without.* Again, it can be seen that Wittgenstein is a sort of existentialist in that the meaningful experience of one's life trumps any philosophical doubts. He would agree with Putnam and other neo-pragmatists that "Ceasing to believe anything at all is not a real human possibility."[206] Again, Wittgenstein writes, ". . . somewhere I must begin with non-doubting; and that is not, so to speak, hasty but excusable . . ."[207] And: ". . . somewhere I must begin with an assumption or a decision."[208] Wittgenstein does not shy

---

[200]   ibid. §1.

[201]   ibid. §192, §212.

[202]   ibid. §245.

[203]   ibid. §577; see also §360, §636, and §663.

[204]   ibid. 577.

[205]   ibid. §360.

[206]   Putnam, Hilary. Pragmatism: An Open Question. 1995. pg. 68.

[207]   On Certainty, §150.

[208]   ibid. §146.

away from this controversial connection between knowledge and decision. In fact, he explicitly embraces the relationship, writing, "But doesn't it come out that knowledge is related to a decision?"[209] And answering, "If someone says that he will recognize no experience as proof of the opposite, that is after all a *decision*."[210]

Of course, not all knowledge is basic knowledge. In addition to contextually basic beliefs, we can also have knowledge of higher order beliefs, which are to some degree supported by our basic ones. For example, (c) *my car is in the parking lot*, is not a contextually basic belief of the language-game. Rather, it is a higher order belief that is supported by a network of language-game beliefs, which include beliefs about perception, memory, causation, etc. In order that I might know that my car is in the parking lot, I may have to appeal to such other beliefs as (d) *when I seemed to see my car in the parking lot a minute ago, my eyes did not deceive me,* (e) *I am correctly remembering what I saw a minute ago, and* (f) *cars cannot vanish into thin air, etc..* So, belief (c) is dependent upon (d), (e), and (f). That is to say a higher order claim can only be as secure as the contextually basic beliefs on which it relies. (I will return to this example momentarily.)

Wittgenstein describes contextual knowledge of higher order beliefs in a number of different ways. He writes, "One says "I know' when one is ready to give compelling grounds."[211] Again: knowledge involves mentioning "how one knows, or at least [being able to] do so."[212] Further:

---

209 ibid. §362.
210 ibid. §368.
211 ibid. §243.
212 ibid. §484.

"Knowledge is . . . based on acknowledgement."[213] Or finally: "If someone says he *knows* something, it must be something that, by general consent, he is in position to know."[214] Thus, contextual knowledge involves being able to give an account of one's justification, being in an appropriate epistemic position, and having both one's account and one's position confirmed or recognized by the epistemic community in general. Wittgenstein believes these three criteria of contextual knowledge are reducible to one broadly conceived criterion. That is, if rational participants in the language-game would assert that my belief is above doubt, then I have contextual knowledge.[215]

The skeptical problem with contextual knowledge is easy to anticipate. According to Wittgenstein, our foundational beliefs and practices are not justified. Thus, it seems that our higher level beliefs are only conditionally secure. They are secure, we can say, if and only if the foundational beliefs upon which they rely are true, but we have no way of testing the truth of these basic beliefs. Remember Wittgenstein's quotation from earlier in the chapter:

> If you do know that *here is one hand,* we'll grant you all the rest. When one says that such and such a proposition can't be proved, of course that does not mean that it can't be derived from other propositions; any proposition can be derived from other ones.

---

213   ibid. §378; see also §18.

214   ibid. §555; see also §551.

215   ibid. §325, §194, §452.

But they may be no more certain than it is itself.[216]

There are a manifold of reasons why the claim (c) *my car is in the parking lot,* might not be true. Perhaps when I thought I saw my car a minute ago, I was being tricked by some mirrors. Perhaps, I have been hallucinating or dreaming. Perhaps, some as yet undiscovered scientific principle has, in fact, made my car vanish. Or perhaps, again, I am, simply a brain being kept alive in the laboratory of a mad scientist, continually being fed fictional experiences.[217] Of course, none of these explanations signify a reasonable doubt, though all are (in some sense) possible. In other words, even if no members of the epistemic community expressed a doubt about (c), it could still be the case that (c) is false. So, a contextually justified belief does not guarantee truth, and since epistemologists have traditionally maintained that knowledge is at minimum a true justified belief, it may or may not be the case that our contextual belief really is knowledge. In other words, we are left with an externalist sort of knowledge, in which it is possible to have knowledge without the knowledge of whether or not one has knowledge, and this is not the sort of knowledge that the contextualists are after.

But Wittgenstein also seems to recognize and comment on another sort of knowledge: that is, traditional knowledge. Although he recognizes such knowledge, he seems to be skeptical that this kind of knowledge can be attained for many external empirical beliefs. Wittgenstein distinguishes contextual knowledge from traditional knowledge, writing,

---

[216]   ibid. §1.

[217]   Pollock, John L. Contemporary Theories of Knowledge, 1986.

"'I know' expresses *comfortable* certainty, not the certainty that is still struggling."[218] What I believe Wittgenstein means by this confusing statement is that *there are two kinds of certainty, related to two kinds of knowledge.* One is comfortable certainty, which is the kind of certainty on which we act in our daily lives. An example of a comfortable certainty might be *if I turn my steering wheel to the left, my car will go left.* I have no good reason for doubting this, and in fact, I don't doubt it. This is evidenced by the fact that I am confident when driving my car. The certainty that is still struggling seems to be theoretical knowledge claims which aim at a *focus imaginarius,* a point of absolute certainty at which we aim, but *may* never reach. Descartes' *cogito* would be an example of a struggling certainty. Any belief which can obtain comfortable certainty is contextual knowledge, but only beliefs which can achieve the certainty that is struggling qualify as traditional epistemic knowledge. This traditional sort of knowledge, struggling certainty, is a belief justified to the point at which we know it to be true. Thus, the traditional kind of knowledge that Wittgenstein discusses is an internalist account — that is to say, if we have traditional knowledge, then we also have knowledge that we have knowledge.

Wittgenstein is clearly skeptical about the possibility of this sort of knowledge (for most external empirical beliefs). He writes, "A judge might . . . say 'That is the truth — so far as a human can know it.'"[219] And again:

> I always feel like saying (although it is wrong): "I know that — so far as one can

---

[218]   On Certainty, §357.

[219]   ibid. §607.

know such a thing." That is incorrect, but something right is hidden behind it.[220]

Although once again a confusing statement, I believe Wittgenstein is trying to express the locution: *I know that in some sense; although of course, I cannot know it in the traditional epistemic sense because the skeptical arguments are too stalwart, but I can know it contextually.*

It is true, of course, that Wittgenstein impugns this latter sort of knowledge. He writes "Forget this transcendent certainty, which is connected to your concept of spirit."[221] But he does not dismiss it because it is an incorrect account of knowledge. Rather, he argues that it proves fruitless and discordant with the concerns of our everyday lives. He writes, "But it isn't that the situation is like this: We just *can't* investigate everything, and for that reason we are forced to rest content with assumption. If I want the door to turn, the hinges must stay put."[222] He continues, "My *life* consists in my being content to accept many things."[223] Thus, Wittgenstein's promotion of contextual knowledge over traditional knowledge is for existential reasons — because it is conducive to living our lives — not for analytically philosophical ones. So, Wittgenstein can be said to be skeptical in an epistemic sense, but anti-skeptical in a pragmatic sense. The result of this bipolar attitude is that he must hold two distinct accounts of knowledge simultaneously, an epistemic account and a pragmatic one.

Some would take issue with the claim that Wittgenstein

---

[220] ibid. §623.

[221] ibid. §42.

[222] ibid. §343.

[223] ibid. §344.

recognizes and, in fact, holds two distinct accounts of knowledge simultaneously: a traditional account of knowledge, with respect to which he is skeptical, and a pragmatic, or existential account of knowledge, which is conducive to our everyday lives, and with respect to which he is anti-skeptical. These critics would argue (1) that Wittgenstein does not keep the traditional account of knowledge. He destroys it and replaces it completely with a new account. And that (2) Wittgenstein is not, in fact, a skeptic in any sense. In what follows, I will attempt to show that my interpretation is tenable and consistent and can withstand these criticisms.

The first objection, that Wittgenstein sets out to destroy the traditional account of knowledge and replace it with contextual knowledge, is the more obdurate one. If I can show that (1) is unfounded, it will not be difficult to get rid of (2), for pundants are in agreement that he does not think the traditional account of knowledge is possible. Ashok Vohra writes that the popular opinion of Wittgenstein is that he "has a corrosive effect in the sense that at the end of a reading of his ideas one is left with nothing positive. It is alleged that Wittgenstein has a destructive mind."[224] Wittgenstein, himself, laments in a diary entry (included in *Culture and Value*), "[A piece of music] came into my head today as I was thinking about my philosophical work and saying to myself: 'I destroy, I destroy, I destroy.'"[225]

However, I do not believe that it is Wittgenstein's intention to destroy the traditional account of knowledge, but merely to

---

[224] Vohra, Ashok. Preface to Wittgenstein's Philosophy of Mind. La Salle: Open Court, 1986.

[225] Wittgenstein, Culture and Value, Peter Winch translation; Chicago: University of Chicago Press, 1980. p. 21e.

assign it to its proper logical space within the language-game of philosophy, and to extricate it from the sphere of everyday practice. Textual evidence that Wittgenstein continues to hold two distinct accounts of knowledge appears at §18 (in *On Certainty*), when Wittgenstein discusses what 'I know' *often* means, not just what it categorically means, at §260 when he clarifies that he will now be using the expression 'I know' as it is used in *normal linguistic exchange*, and at §184, §343, §607, which were discussed earlier. But there seems to be a more subtle, and also more deeply cutting argument to show that Wittgenstein holds two accounts of knowledge simultaneously.

Previously, I showed how Wittgenstein believed that knowledge was necessarily connected with doubt. To be known is to be above doubt. But what sort of doubt? Wittgenstein makes a distinction between two types of doubts, *necessary* and *possible doubt.* He writes, "What I need to shew is that a doubt is not necessary even when it is possible."[226] We can understand Wittgenstein's *necessary doubt* to be the same as Peirce's or David Annis' *real doubt.* Peirce writes that doubt is the result of "some surprising phenomenon, some experience which either disappoints an expectation, or breaks in upon some habit of expectation."[227] Annis, borrowing from Peirce and James, defines a real doubt as a questioning caused by a jar or hitch in one's actual life.[228] Because this is such an important distinction, let me illustrate with a example:

Suppose a surgeon needs to make a particular sort of

---

[226] On Certainty, §392.

[227] Charles S. Peirce, Collected Papers, Vol. 6, edited by C. Hartshorne and P. Weiss. Harvard, 1965. pg. 469.

[228] Annis, p. 205.

incision in an operation, and confers with a colleague. He need not answer the objection that we don't really *know* if a sharp scalpel will incise the body or that the patient may be a space alien with a different internal structure. In fact, if one did make these objections, she would likely be thrown out of the operating room. Such doubts are not the product of any jar or hitch in our actual life, and they do not represent any genuine concerns. In other words, they are *possible,* but in no way *necessary* doubts. However, if a qualified physician objects that the surgeon's proposed point of incision is too high or that the scalpel is of the wrong kind for the surgery, or that the patient is a hemophiliac and special precautions need to be taken with the incision, then the surgeon must address these objections. They are genuine, pragmatic concerns which must be taken into consideration. These are *real* doubts.

Another way to make the distinction is to say that necessary doubts are doubts which have a grounding in experience. Possible doubts need no such grounding. When Wittgenstein writes, "Can I doubt it? Grounds for doubt are lacking! Everything speaks in its favour, nothing against it. Nevertheless, it is imaginable . . .,"[229] he is saying simply that there are no necessary doubts here, although of course, there are possible doubts. There are always possible doubts.[230]

If knowledge is necessarily connected to doubt, such that what is known is what is above doubt, and if there are two kinds of doubt, it would follow that there are also, then, two types of knowledge, a knowledge that is beyond necessary, or reasonable doubt, that is contextual knowledge, and a

---

[229] On Certainty, §4.
[230] ibid. §117, §122, §322.

knowledge that is beyond possible, or philosophical doubt, that is traditional epistemic knowledge.

Of course, it does not follow that Wittgenstein embraces or advocates each equally. In fact, it is part of my argument that far from embracing traditional knowledge, he is skeptical about the very possibility of it, that is to say, he thinks it may be impossible to rid ourselves of all possible doubts.

Wittgenstein is skeptical that either our contextually basic beliefs or our higher order beliefs can be above possible doubt. Regarding basic beliefs, he writes, in the voice of an imaginary interlocutor, "'It is certain that we didn't arrive on this planet from another one . . . [a] hundred years ago.'" And responds, "Well, it's as certain as such things are."[231] He writes further, "I cannot say that I have good grounds for the opinion that cats do not grow on trees or that I had a father and a mother."[232] Elsewhere, he writes that he is not satisfied of the correctness of his most basic beliefs.[233] Such basic beliefs as those about the origins of cats and human beings are not above *possible* doubt.

Further, higher order beliefs are not above possible doubt. He writes, "if what he believes is of such a kind that the grounds that he can give are no surer than his assertion, then he cannot say that he knows what he believes."[234] In other words, if our contextually basic beliefs are insecure, then the higher order beliefs upon which they rest are, likewise, insecure. He gives an example of what he means, writing,

---

[231]   ibid. §184

[232]   ibid. §282.

[233]   ibid. §94.

[234]   ibid. §243.

> It would strike me as ridiculous to want
> to doubt the existence of Napoleon; but if
> someone doubted the existence of the earth
> 150 years ago, perhaps I should be more
> willing to listen, for now he is doubting our
> whole system of evidence. It does not strike
> me as if this system were more certain than
> a certainty within it.[235]

Higher order beliefs cannot be more secure than contextually basic beliefs. And contextually basic beliefs are not above all possible doubt. Since by traditional knowledge, Wittgenstein means beliefs above all possible doubt, he must, therefore, be skeptical about the possibility of traditional knowledge, both for basic and higher order empirical beliefs. Wittgenstein chooses to ultimately replace absolute, unassailable, traditional knowledge with the only kind of knowledge that is possible and meaningful, contextual knowledge, which is conditional and not indubitable. While it's certainly true that Wittgenstein ultimately promotes contextual knowledge in his later work, he still maintains and discusses the traditional account of knowledge (that of his teachers, Moore and Russell,) and of its failure in the epistemological arena.[236]

---

[235] ibid. §185.

[236] Some support for my biperspectival reading of Wittgenstein's use of the word 'knowledge' can be found in Part II, Section X of the Philosophical Investigations. There, Wittgenstein distinguishes two usages of the word 'believe.' He writes, "Similarly: the statement 'I believe it's going to rain' has a meaning like, that is to say a use like, 'It's going to rain,' but the meaning of 'I believed then that it was going to rain', is

Section 2.7: Epistemic Contextualism Defined

Although Wittgenstein admits, "I am trying to say something that sounds like pragmatism,"[237] his theory in fact, represents a different sort of response to the regress problem. While pragmatists maintain that the regress is avoided because beliefs can be immediately *justified* by their utility, Wittgenstein argues that we have logically foundational beliefs, but they can have no justification as such. He writes, "This game proves its worth. That may be the cause of its being played, *but it is not the grounds*."[238] Both the pragmatist and the contextualist are appealing to existential reasons for their most basic beliefs, but only the pragmatists are suggesting that our foundational beliefs are justified through their practical utility. The contextualist maintains that while we do not have justification for our basic beliefs, it is rational to act as if we did.

So, straight away, we should be able to see that epistemic contextualists reject (1) that *we can avoid the regress problem of inferential justification because our beliefs are immediately justified or unjustified based on the practical difference their veracity would make in life.* But what about the other principles, (2) and (3)? Although there is some debate concerning Wittgenstein's theory of truth (Wittgenstein, himself, being less than explicit on this point), there seems to be little evidence to suggest that the contextualist theory wholly rejects the distinction between truth and justification.

---

not like that of 'It did rain then'." Wittgenstein, Philosophical Investigations, p. 190e.

[237] On Certainty, §422.

[238] ibid. §474; italics added.

In fact, D. B. Annis, another contextualist, firmly offers, "the contextualist account . . . does not ignore the distinction between truth and justification."[239] Further, I think it is clear that contextualism embraces the distinction between appearance and reality. This is shown by the fact that Wittgenstein acknowledges that one may be wrong about a sensational belief: "Could I say 'I know the positions of my hands with my eyes closed' if the position I gave always or mostly contradicted the evidence of other people?"[240] Wittgenstein answers *no*. What my senses tell me may not correspond with the evidence of others. It may be objected that I am overstating this distinction. If so, I am willing to assert this lesser position: that (2) and (3) are not claims that are necessarily made by contextualists or essential to contextualism.

In these two sections, I think I have successfully shown that epistemic contextualism has many salient points of differentiation with epistemic pragmatism. While the pragmatist theory of knowledge argues that our foundational beliefs are *justified*, contextualism argues that they *are not*. Thus, contextualists do not agree on the *first* essential principle of epistemic pragmatism. Further, epistemic pragmatism denies the distinction between appearance and reality, which the contextualist still maintains. Thus, contextualists and pragmatists disagree about the *third* essential principle of epistemic pragmatism. Finally, I find little evidence to believe that contextualists reject the distinction between truth and justification that is rejected by pragmatism. Thus, it seems that the contextualist, unlike the pragmatist *may allow* for the existence of recognition-transcendent truths

---

[239] Annis. p. 210.

[240] On Certainty, §502.

(that is to say, it may be possible that there is a true statement which is not known by anyone) and that contextualists, likewise, deny the *second* essential principle of epistemic pragmatism. These are poignant disagreements. Therefore, I think it is now clear that epistemic pragmatism and epistemic contextualism constitute distinct existential paradigms of knowledge.

But is epistemic contextualism now defined? I think I have indeed differentiated it from epistemic pragmatism, and in so doing, I consider the central part of my project for this chapter to be completed. Like pragmatism, contextualism eludes easy categorization and analytic definition according to essential features. But like I did in my study of pragmatism, I would like to point out three features common to contextualists (and uncommon to pragmatists) which I believe are central tenets of the theory. First, unlike pragmatism and indeed, all other paradigms of justification, the epistemic contextualist holds that (A) the regress of inferential beliefs terminates with beliefs that are logically foundational, but not epistemically so; in other words, it ends with beliefs which are contextually basic, beliefs which lie beyond being epistemically justified or unjustified and provide only contingent justification to the edifice of empirical knowledge. Further, contextualists hold that (B) truth is not necessarily identical to justification. And, (C) that appearance is not necessarily identical to reality. These two conditions may be seen as one – that contextualists do not necessarily accept an exclusively pragmatist or phenomenal metaphysics

In this chapter, I have distinguished two existential paradigms of justification – epistemic pragmatism and epistemic contextualism. I began by exploring the largely untracked relationship between William James and

Ludwig Wittgenstein. Next, I explored pragmatism in depth, defending it against some obdurate misreadings, presenting an early attempt at defining it according to three analytic criteria, critiquing that attempt, and finally giving a more subtle and sophisticated elucidation of pragmatist epistemology which included a discussion of how the classical pragmatists reconstructed the traditional notions of truth and knowledge. Next, I explored the theory of epistemic contextualism. This involved an explication of the theory of knowledge of the later Wittgenstein set out in *On Certainty* and (to a lesser extent) *Philosophical Investigations, Culture and Value,* and *The Blue and Brown Books.* Of note in this section is a critical look at his notions of the *language game* and his two uses of the term "knowledge." Finally, I elucidated epistemic contextualism, pointing out three central and distinguishing features. In Chapter 3, I will attempt to codify many so-called "neo-pragmatists" according to the distinction made in this chapter between epistemic pragmatism and contextualism. Also, I will address several important objections to my project, specifically and in general.

CHAPTER THREE

I N THE FIRST chapter of this book, I distinguished the four leading paradigms of justification – epistemic foundationalism, coherentism, pragmatism, and contextualism. I dubbed epistemic foundationalism and epistemic coherentism the "traditional paradigms of justification" because they have been the most widely held throughout the history of western philosophy. (Foundationalism has been the most popular theory of justification by far, but in the 20th century, many important thinkers like Bonjour, DeRose, and Lehrer turned to epistemic coherentism.) Epistemic pragmatism and epistemic contextualism have been less popular historically although they have had vigorous and important advocates. I take the mature work of William James and John Dewey to be representative of epistemic pragmatism and the later work of Ludwig Wittgenstein to be paradigmatic of epistemic contextualism. Together, I refer to pragmatism and contextualism as the "existential paradigms of justification" due to their reliance on practical, humanistic methods. In Chapter One, I explicated each of the four theories of justification, provided arguments (some popular and some original) against foundationalism and coherentism and gave evidence for my belief that the existential paradigms offered a more eminent, more hopeful, and practically superior alternative to the traditional paradigms.

In Chapter Two, I explored epistemic pragmatism and epistemic contextualism in greater depth, elucidating each and distinguishing them from each other. Among the important tenets of epistemic pragmatism I pointed out were the following: pragmatists (1) *avoid the regress problem of inferential justification by arguing that our beliefs are immediately justified or unjustified based on the practical difference their veracity would make in life.* (2) Pragmatists hold *that there is no distinction between truth and justification (or that truth is defined in justificatory terms.)* And finally they hold (3), *that there is no distinction between the world and the world as we perceive and interact with it.* I likewise elucidated epistemic contextualism, pointing out three distinguishing tenets: Epistemic contextualists hold that: (A) *the regress of inferential justification is terminated by beliefs which are logically but not epistemically basic, beliefs which lie beyond being epistemically justified or unjustified and supply only contingent justification to the edifice of empirical knowledge.* We call these beliefs contextually basic beliefs. (B) *Contextualists reject the pragmatist idea that there is no distinction between truth and justification – that they are one and the same enterprise.* And (C) *epistemic contextualists reject the pragmatist idea that appearance and reality are indistinct, that reality is the phenomenal.*

At this time, I would like to make the distinction between epistemic pragmatism and epistemic contextualism clearer with an illustration. Epistemic pragmatism and epistemic contextualism are very similar. They both emphasize methods which are social, practical, contingent, and human.

One of the best ways to tell an epistemic pragmatist from an epistemic contextualist is to look at their stance on justification. Pragmatists hold that our most basic beliefs are justified by their practical utility. If it makes sense to *treat* a belief as justified, then that belief *is* justified, because it is meaningless to hold onto a distinction which does not make a practical difference. This is not necessarily the case for contextualists. They do not take their most basic beliefs as justified. It may make sense to treat them as justified or to act as though they were justified, but this is not the same as being justified. Contextualists do not necessarily accept the pragmatic rule that says any difference that does not make a difference is not really a difference at all.

Consider this story: An unarmed man is running away from some enemies heavily armed with swords and spears. Eventually, he comes to a great chasm in the earth, which he cannot possibly go around. He is greatly outnumbered, so to turn and fight would be suicide. His only hope of survival is to leap over the chasm. He does not have justification to believe he could leap that far but he knows from his study of psychology that if he *believes* he can leap over the chasm he will have a better chance of *actually* leaping over the chasm. So he forces himself to believe for the moment that the chasm jump is possible. Whether the man makes it or not is not our present concern. What is relevant is that for the epistemic pragmatist, this man who has chosen to believe he can jump the chasm *is* now justified. He is justified because it is practically helpful to act as though he is justified and there is no relevance to making a distinction between what he is justified in believing and what is practically helpful for him to believe he is justified in believing. The contextualist does not view this man's willed belief as justified. Perhaps it is practically rational to treat this belief as justified for the moment, but this does not make it actually justified. This is a poignant difference between pragmatism and contextualism and the recognition of this difference will help us with our main project in Chapter Three.

SECTION 3.1: NEO-PRAGMATISM

In this chapter, I will be codifying some of the philosophers who have been referred to from time to time as *neo-pragmatists* according to the distinctions I have made in Chapters One and Two. Let's begin by seeing which thinkers have been dubbed "neo-pragmatists." The first mention of the term "neo-pragmatism" that I have found in my literature search appeared as the title of R. J. Richman's 1956 paper, "Neo-Pragmatism." In this paper, he coins the term in order to refer to the new empiricist philosophy set forth by Professor Willard Quine in his seminal 1951 article, "Two Dogmas of Empiricism."[241] Richman writes, "Quine proceeds to indicate what empiricism would be like without

---

[241] "Professor Willard Quine's provocative article "Two Dogmas of Empiricism" has given rise to a considerable amount of discussion, most of it devoted to Quine's contention that the maintenance of a sharp distinction between analytic and synthetic statements is an unfounded supposition, a "dogma" of empiricists. The other "dogma" referred to in the title of Quine's essay is that of "reductionism", i.e. in general, the doctrine that individual statements are confirmable or infirmable in experience. One particular form of this doctrine is represented by "the verification theory of meaning", which equates the meaning of a statement with the method of empirically confirming or disconfirming it. R. J. Richman. "Neo-Pragmatism." Methodos, Volume 8. 1956. pp. 35-46. p. 35.

[dogmas], and it is this 'empiricism without dogmas,' which I shall call *neo-pragmatism* . . .."[242] Richman continues, "Neo-pragmatism represents an attempt to divest empiricism entirely of *a priorism* by rendering *all* our knowledge subject to empirical control."[243] Ironically, W. V. Quine is not one of the central figures now associated with neo-pragmatism. In his article, "Reconstruction in Pragmatism," Joseph Margolis enumerates several thinkers whom he calls neo-pragmatists. Among these are Hilary Putnam, Richard Rorty, Ludwig Wittgenstein, "the pre-Kehre Martin Heidegger, the original Ralph Waldo Emerson," and "W. V. Quine very marginally . . .."[244] Others that have often been referred to as neo-pragmatists are William Alston, David Annis, Donald Davidson, Karl-Otto Apel, Jürgen Habermas, Wilfrid Sellars, and Robert Brandom.[245] In this book, I will critically consider the epistemologies of Rorty, Annis, Alston, and Putnam, and to a briefer and less thorough

---

[242] R. J. Richman. "Neo-Pragmatism." Methodos, Volume 8. 1956. pp. 35-46. p. 35.

[243] ibid. 36.

[244] Joseph Margolis, "Reconstruction in Pragmatism," Journal of Speculative Philosophy, Volume 13, Number 4. 1999. pp. 221-238. p. 221.

[245] see Joseph Margolis's "Reconstruction in Pragmatism," Journal of Speculative Philosophy, Volume 13, Number 4. 1999. pp. 221-238. p. 221. And: Joseph Margolis's "Richard Rorty: Philosophy by Other Means", Journal of Speculative Philosophy, Volume 13, Number 4. 1999. pp. 221-238. Another source I am drawing from in listing thinkers who have been called "neo-pragmatists" is the reading list for a seminar entitled "Neo-Pragmatism" taught by James Bohman, which I attended as a graduate student at Saint Louis University.

extent, Quine and Brandom. Let us begin by taking a close look at the existential epistemlogy of Richard Rorty.

Section 3.2: Richard Rorty Considered

Rorty is considered by many to be one of the central figures of neo-pragmatism. Joseph Margolis writes, "If pragmatism began with James's strong misreading of Peirce, it came to life again with Rorty's strong misreading of Dewey, whom [Rorty] described as a 'postmodernist before his time.'"[246] In his article, "Universality and Truth," appearing in the 2000 book, *Rorty and His Critics,*[247] edited by Robert Brandom, Rorty refers to himself six times as a pragmatist, twice as a Deweyan, and four times as a coherentist.[248] In one paragraph, he refers to himself as a pragmatist in one sentence and as a coherentist in the next, strongly suggesting that he does not distinguish the epistemological paradigms in the same way I do. Rorty is generally accepted among the philosophical community as a member of the new generation of pragmatists. But it is not obvious that Rorty is a pragmatist, or even that he considers himself a pragmatist in the way I have been using the term in this book. Margolis writes, "Had not Rorty and Putnam identified themselves as pragmatists . . . no one would have

---

[246] Joseph Margolis, "Reconstruction in Pragmatism," Journal of Speculative Philosophy, Volume 13, Number 4. 1999. pp. 221-238. p. 221.

[247] Rorty and His Critics, Edited by Robert Brandom, Blackwell, 2000.

[248] He writes, for example, "We pragmatists . . .." (p. 15), "Pragmatists like me . . .." (p. 13), "Deweyans like myself . . .." (7), "We coherentists . . .." (5), etc..

envisaged a 'revival.'"[249] But Rorty describes himself in a number of ways – as a pragmatist, a coherentist, and a *post-modernist*.[250] Also, he shares a great deal with Wittgenstein and the contextualists, (even describing himself as an *admirer* of the later Wittgenstein[251]) for instance his insistence upon the centrality of social, linguistic practices. He writes, "I think Habermas is absolutely right that we need to *socialize* and *linguistify* the notion of 'reason' by viewing it as communicative."[252] He continues,

> Perhaps the most far-reaching difference between Habermas and me is that [I] sympathize with the anti-metaphysical, 'postmodern', thinkers he criticizes when they suggest that the idea of a distinction between social practice and what transcends such practice is an undesirable remnant of logocentrism. Foucault and Dewey can agree that, whether or not inquiry is always a matter of 'power', it never transcends social practice. Both would say that the only thing that can transcend a social practice is another social practice.[253]

To understand Rorty's theory of knowledge, I think it is important to understand what he means when he identifies

---

[249]   Margolis, 1999. p. 222. See also, Margolis, 2000. p. 532.

[250]   Rorty, "Universality and Truth," Rorty and His Critics. Edited by Robert Brandom, Blackwell, 2000. p. 7. See also Margolis, 1999, p.223 and 226, and Margolis, 2000, p. 530.

[251]   Putnam, 1995. p. 64.

[252]   Rorty, "Universality and Truth," p. 2.

[253]   ibid. 7.

himself as a post-modernist. The term 'post-modernism' like the term 'existentialism' a few decades ago, is now so broadly used not only in philosophy, but also in the arenas of art, literature, and education that it has virtually lost all meaning by taking on so many different meanings. When used by Rorty to refer to his own position, he seems to mean the rejection or at least the deep suspicion of three epistemological and metaphysical premises which are accepted by the majority of Anglo-American thinkers. He writes,

> One of the desires said to be universal by philosophers interested in democratic politics is the desire for truth. In the past, such philosophers have typically conjoined the claim that there is universal human agreement on the supreme desirability of truth with two further premises: that truth is correspondence to reality, and that reality has an intrinsic nature (that there is, in Nelson Goodman's terms, a Way the World Is). Given these three premises, they proceed to argue that Truth is One, and that the universal human interest in truth provides motive for creating an inclusivist community. The more of that truth we uncover, the more common ground we shall share, and the more tolerant and inclusivist we shall therefore become. The rise of relatively democratic, relatively tolerant, societies in the last few hundred years is said to be due to the increased rationality of modern times, where 'rationality' denotes

the employment of an innate truth-oriented
faculty.[254]

These three premises, that truth is universally desired, that truth is a relation of correspondence between a proposition and reality, and that there is an absolute reality which may be corresponded to, constitute the basic core of epistemology and metaphysics for the standard western thinker. And it is the rejection (or suspicion) of these core beliefs that constitutes a post-modern viewpoint for Rorty. He writes in the Introduction to his 1998 collection, *Truth and Progress*, "[I will] argue that philosophy will get along better without the notions of 'the intrinsic nature of reality' and 'correspondence to reality' than with them."[255] Given his affirmation of this view he calls post-modernism, we can very likely guess how Rorty will fall in terms of our new distinction between epistemic pragmatism and contextualism. But rather than settling for an educated guess, let's find, in Rorty's own words, his position on the foundations of knowledge, on appearance and reality, and on truth and justification.

As I have stated a number of times already in the book, the epistemic pragmatist believes that justification is a matter of practical utility. If believing that a certain belief p is justified is helpful and utilitarian, then p is justified. Rorty agrees with James that "'the good in the way of belief' and 'what is better for us to believe' are interchangeable with 'justified' . . .."[256] And this is how the regress of inferential

---

[254] ibid. 1.

[255] Rorty, Introduction to Truth and Progress: Philosophical Papers, Volume 3 Cambridge University Press, 1998. p. 2.

[256] ibid. 2.

beliefs is brought to an end. In "Universality and Truth," Rorty gives a nice illustration of the instrumental nature of justification:

> My problem with Wellmer, Apel, and Habermas is that I do not see what the pragmatic force of saying that an argument which, like most other arguments, convinces certain people and not others is a "good argument." This seems like saying that a tool which, like all tools, is useful for a certain purpose but not others, is a good tool. Imagine the surgeon saying, after unsuccessfully attempting to dig a tunnel out of his prison cell with his scalpel, "Still, it's a good tool." Then picture him saying, after unsuccessfully trying to argue his guards into letting him escape so that he may resume his position as leader of the resistance, "Still, they were good arguments."[257]

"There is no such thing," Rorty claims, "as a belief being justified *sans phrase* – justified once and for all . . .."[258] In his article, "Richard Rorty on Reality and Justification," Hilary Putnam also recognizes Rorty's view of justification as situational, practical, and sociological.[259] So, in regard to criterion (1), the justification of basic beliefs, Rorty

---

[257] Rorty, "Universality and Truth," p. 9.

[258] Rorty, Introduction to Truth and Progress: Philosophical Papers, Volume 3 Cambridge University Press, 1998. p. 2.

[259] Hilary Putnam, "Richard Rorty on Reality and Justification," Rorty and His Critics. Edited by Robert Brandom, Blackwell, 2000. p. 84.

clearly seems to agree with the epistemic pragmatists. But what about criteria (2) and (3)? The second criteria of epistemic pragmatism was that truth is seen as indistinct from justification, or alternately that truth was construed as a kind of justification or the product of justification. Again, Rorty agrees with the classical pragmatists. In his 1995 article, "Is Truth a Goal of Inquiry? Donald Davidson versus Crispin Wright," he claims that "Philosophers, who like myself, find this Jamesian suggestion persuasive, swing back and forth between trying to reduce truth to justification and propounding some form of minimalism about truth."[260] Elsewhere he writes that pragmatists are "suspicious of the distinction between truth and justification,"[261] and finally, that, "only over attention to fact-stating would make one think that there was an aim of inquiry called 'truth' in addition to that of justification."[262] A corollary of the rejection of the distinction between truth and justification is that there is no context-transcendent truth, or more precisely, that the idea of a context-transcendent truth is meaningless and confused. Rorty writes, "My problem is intensified when I ask myself whether my truth claims 'transcend my local cultural context.' I have no clear idea whether they do or not, because I cannot see what 'transcendence means here."[263] And: "For assertions such as 'Clinton is the better candidate,' 'Alexander came before Ceasar,' 'Gold is insoluble in hydrochloric acid,' it is hard to see why I should

---

[260]   Rorty, "Is Truth a Goal of Inquiry? Donald Davidson versus Crispin Wright," Philosophical Quarterly, Volume 45, July 1995. Truth and Progress, Cambridge University Press, 1998. p. 20.

[261]   ibid. 19.

[262]   Rorty, "Universality and Truth," p. 3.

[263]   ibid. p. 9.

ask myself 'is my claim context-dependent or universal?' No difference to practice is made by coming down in favor of one alternative rather than the other."[264]

Since Richard Rorty accepts the three distinguishing features I have associated with epistemic pragmatism, it is my judgment that Rorty (perhaps to little surprise) should be regarded as an epistemic pragmatist. Let us now turn to a tougher case and look at the complex existential epistemology of David B. Annis.

SECTION 3.3: DAVID ANNIS CONSIDERED

Again, Annis is a student of the philosophy of Peirce as well as Wittgenstein, and has a great deal in common with the classical pragmatists. But it is my contention that Annis should be classed as an epistemic contextualist according to my distinction. Let us remember the distinguishing features of contextualism: (A) contextualists resolve the regress problem of inferential justification by appealing to contextually basic beliefs, beliefs which are beyond being justified or unjustified and supply only conditional justification on higher order beliefs. Further, (B) contextualists do not necessarily accept the pragmatist idea that truth and justification are indistinct. And finally, (C) contextualists do not necessarily agree with the pragmatist idea that appearance and reality are indistinct. In this section, I will spell out Annis's unique theory of knowledge, finally pointing to his agreement with the criteria above.

Although Annis does not claim to be revising or finishing Wittgenstein's epistemic project, I believe his 1978 article, "A Contextualist Theory of Epistemic Justification,"

---

[264]   ibid. p. 6.

takes off right where Wittgenstein's *On Certainty* ends. Like Wittgenstein, Annis maintains that the regress of inferential justification is terminated by *contextually basic beliefs*.[265] These are foundational empirical beliefs which are not epistemically justified. However, they support (conditionally) the remainder of our edifice of empirical knowledge. Further, Annis agrees with Wittgenstein that all justification for non-basic beliefs is either inferred from contextually basic beliefs or socially acquired through pragmatic testing. (I will explicate the method of this testing momentarily.) His theory's primary epistemic goal is truth[266], which he does not associate with what is most expedient or utilitarian. Finally, like Wittgenstein, Annis' epistemology offers that it is possible to have *contextual* knowledge without access to truth. (Contextual knowledge is merely a justified belief, and is therefore fallible.) The primary difference between Annis and the later Wittgenstein, is, I believe, that Annis's theory is more sophisticated and complete. For example, while Wittgenstein neglects to spell out in precise terms the manner of the pragmatic testing of beliefs, Annis gives us a thorough account of this procedure. He tells us exactly how it is to be conducted and by whom.

The successful passing of a pragmatic knowledge test, says Annis, rests in being able to meet certain objections of an epistemic community relative to our collective epistemic goals. These goals include the maximization of explanatory power, simplicity, and the conservation of existing beliefs.

---

[265] David B. Annis, "A Contextualist Theory of Epistemic Justification," Empirical Knowledge: Readings in Contemporary Epistemology. Edited by Paul K. Moser. Rowman & Littlefield, 1986. p. 203, 208.

[266] ibid. p. 204.

However, these three goals are only "subsidiary to the goals of [having true beliefs and avoiding false ones.]"[267] What is the nature of these objections that must be met for a non-basic belief to be justified? And how are these objections to be addressed? Annis spells out four conditions for good pragmatic testing. First, the objection must be a product of a real doubt;[268] second, it must be answered relative to what Annis calls an *issue-context;*[269] third, it must arise from an appropriate *objector-group;*[270] and fourth, the objection must be of one of two types of proper objections. (I will enumerate these later in this section.)

A *real doubt,* Annis claims is a doubt which is caused by a *jar or hitch* in someone's actual life.[271] Annis cites Peirce, who writes that "doubt is an uneasy and dissatisfied state from which we struggle to free ourselves" and that it is the result of "some surprising phenomenon, some experience which either disappoints an expectation, or breaks in upon some habit of expectation."[272] Also, a real doubt is one which is assigned a significant probability by the objector and the rest of the objector-group. A merely hypothetical doubt, which is not the result of a surprising experience and which would be assigned a very low probability by the epistemic community would not qualify as a proper objection to anyone's belief. Some justificatory questions are, of course, more important than others. For example, "Is this unconscious patient a diabetic?" may be more important than the question, "who composed this symphony?" Annis

---

[267] ibid. p. 204.

[268] ibid. p. 204-5.

[269] ibid. p. 205-6.

[270] ibid. p. 206.

[271] ibid. p. 205.

[272] ibid. p. 205.

maintains that the stakes of knowing differ from situation to situation, and consequently the level of support needed to obtain the status of contextual justification likewise varies. We may need to be much more careful when deciding how to proceed in treating this patient's medical condition than whether the music we are listening to was written by Schumann or Prokofiev.

The importance of a justificatory question and the corresponding amount of justification needed for a particular belief are aspects of what Annis calls the *issue-context*. The issue-context can be compared to Wittgenstein's language-game. Annis writes, "The issue-context is what specific issue . . . is being raised. It determines the level of understanding and knowledge that [one] must exhibit, and it determines the appropriate objector-group."[273] To ensure that proper objections (i.e. relevant objections which spring from real doubts) are raised, one must consult with a proper epistemic community, or as Annis calls it, *objector-group*. The objector-group is that group of peers that is best suited for raising objections and confirming justificatory questions relative to a given issue-context.[274] If the issue is a medical one, the appropriate objector-group would likely be constituted of physicians, nurses, and other medical professionals. If the issue is philosophical, perhaps philosophy professors would comprise the objector-group. In most ordinary situations, however, members of an objector-group need not have any special training or qualifications. Consider the example of a man looking for a red chair to replace a broken one in his house. Nearly anyone would pass as an appropriate objector-group member in this situation. So long as one could tell a

---

[273]   ibid. p. 206.

[274]   ibid. p. 206.

red chair from say an orange chair or a red table, they are qualified. Further, probably nothing of great importance rests on this man finding his red chair. Probably, anyone who happens to be in the store at the time could serve as an appropriate objector-group.

Although the specific criteria for membership in an objector-group sometimes vary from one issue-context to another, there is one thing that all good objector-groups must have in common. They must be composed entirely of what Annis calls *critical truth seekers* or *verifically motivated objectors.* Critical truth seekers are simply people who have as their epistemic goals the finding of true beliefs and the avoidance of false ones. (Notice Annis's insistence on truth and falsity as real properties which are not identical with what is or is not justified.) Only such a person will raise proper objections – that is, relevant objections that are the product of real doubts.[275]

Finally, proper objections are always one of two types. One may object (a) that a subject, S, is not in a good position to know the belief in question, h; or (b) that the belief, h, is false. In many situations, like the one involving the man and his red chair, there will be no objection. The belief that the man has found a red chair may be contextually basic for it seems absurd to ask why this man thinks he has found a red chair. However, even in this situation, it is possible for an objector-group to challenge and even overturn this seemingly basic belief. For example, a critical truth seeking objector might suggest that there is a red light shining on the chair and the chair may really not be red at all. Or the objector might

---

[275] Interestingly and perhaps alarmingly, a critic such as David Hume may not be an qualified objector in Annis' system as the doubts he raising may not be seen as real doubts.

remind the forgetful man that he is color-blind or that he is wearing red-tinted contact lenses. In response to the first objection, our chair buyer could retort that he knows about the light and that he saw the chair yesterday in normal light. In this case, it seems he has successfully met the objection and the belief is contextually justified. If the objector-group had no appropriate objections, the man might also have been contextually justified.

Let us suppose, however, that the belief a person, S, is hoping to justify is not contextually basic. In this case, the objector-group may ask S for her reasons for believing that h. S might respond by giving reasons e1, e2, . . . en for the truth of h. A member of the group may presently object (A) that she is not in good position to know h, or (B) that h is false. Let's suppose that the objecting member makes a type (A) objection: He might object that one of her reasons for believing h is false, or that e1-en does not provide adequate evidence for the truth of h, or that there is some evidence i which counters the belief that h or one of the beliefs e1-en supporting the truth of h. S is now required to address all of these objections provided they are products of real doubts. To meet an objection, S must respond in such a way as to convince the objector-group that the objection k is false or that given k, h is still probably true. S may do this by diminishing the status of k (say, by showing that k only slightly decreases the support for one of S's supporting beliefs, and that h is still justified), or by objecting that k is not an objection of type (A) or (B) and is thus, illegitimate, or that k is not a product of a real doubt. S could also ask the objectors for their reasons for their belief that k, and may offer (A) or (B) type objections to their reasons for the truth of k. This process is carried out in a dialectical fashion until S and the objector-group are in accord. Once again, this social justification will only work if S and all of the members of the objector-group are critical truth seekers.

An important point about the meeting of these objections is that S need not meet all possible real objections to h. This would require S and the members of the objector-group to be in a superior epistemic position than the one they are presently in; but this requirement is too strong. (In some cases, we do require a person to be in the best epistemic position pragmatically possible. However, even this is not usually necessary.) It is easy to imagine that at some future time there will be some new evidence which would disprove h, or show h to be problematic; however, the question of concern for Annis is not whether h is ultimately and forever justified, but rather simply whether h is justified here and now. So, contextual justification is temporally relative. Of course, it is also societally or culturally relative (inasmuch as a language-game or issue-context can be said to belong to a society or culture.) For example, it may be contextually justified in one part of the world that acupuncture has medical value and it may be justified elsewhere that it does not. This does not mean that for contextualists it is true that acupuncture has medical value in one part of the world and false that it has medical value in another part.

Annis gives us a test for contextual justification. He calls this the excusability test. We simply ask whether in a given situation, if S is wrong about her belief that p, would she be epistemically excused. If so, then she was contextually justified. If not, she was not. Let's look at an illustration of this principle. Suppose Smith wishes to know if his friend, Jones, is at this party. He wishes to know merely because he enjoys Jones's company and would like to chat with him. Smith walks from room to room and asks a few people if they have seen Jones. All reply that they have not.

Smith is now justified that Jones is not at the party. This is evidenced by the fact that if Jones were at the party, say hiding in the cloak room, Smith would surely be excused for his mistake. Now let's change the example. Brown, an FBI agent wishes to know if Green, a dangerous criminal is at this party. If Brown merely walks from room to room and asks a few people whether they have seen Green, Brown is not necessarily justified in believing that Green is not at the party. If it turns out that Green is hiding in the cloak room, we would probably not excuse Brown for his error. The stakes have changed, and so the conditions for justification have changed. The test of excusability is relative depending upon the situation and importance of the belief in question.

Now that we have explicated David Annis's theory of knowledge, it should be clear that he is an epistemic contextualist and not an epistemic pragmatist. First, for Annis, the regress of inferential justification is terminated by contextually basic beliefs, beliefs which do not obtain the status of epistemic justification, and offer only contingent or conditional support for higher order beliefs. Also, Annis does not accept pragmatist metaphysics. For Annis, the goal of inquiry is truth, which is not the same as justification. Nor is truth defined in terms of justification or verification processes. And we can see from his insistence upon the members of an objector-group being critical truth seekers that he believes there is a noumenal reality, a way the world is, which is distinct from appearance. Let's now turn to another thinker, who is commonly referred to as a "neo-pragmatist", William Alston.

SECTION 3.4: WILLIAM ALSTON CONSIDERED

In several of his works, William P. Alston acknowledges a debt to Thomas Reid and Ludwig Wittgenstein, but he acknowledges the debt to Wittgenstein grudgingly.[276] In this section, I will look at Alston's "doxastic practice" approach to epistemology, along the way pointing out the wide agreements with Wittgenstein's notion of the language-game. As I proceed, it will be necessary to briefly defend Wittgenstein from some allegations by Alston, which Alston believes distinguishes his theory from Wittgenstein's. I will conclude by suggesting that Alston's epistemology is more similar to Wittgenstein than he is eager to admit, and that Alston's theory of knowledge qualifies as a brand of epistemic contextualism.

The reader should remember how I claimed that Wittgenstein's theory of knowledge was motivated by the existential need to avoid skepticism. Alston's unique approach to epistemology appears to be motivated by similar concerns. In *The Reliability of Sense Perception,* Alston writes, "when we reflect on our epistemic situation, we can hardly turn our backs *on our inability to give a satisfactory demonstration of* [sense perception] *and other doxastic practices."*[277] And in *Perceiving God,* he concludes, "Hence what alternative is there to employing the practices we find ourselves using, to which we find ourselves firmly committed, and which we could abandon or replace only with extreme difficulty

---

[276] See for example, William P. Alston, The Reliability of Sense Perception. Ithica, NY: Cornell University Press, 1993. p. 130; and Alston, "A 'Doxastic Practice' Approach to Epistemology," Knowledge and Skepticism. Edited by Marjorie Clay and Keith Lehrer. Boulder, CO: Westview Press, 1989. pp. 4-13.

[277] Alston, 1993. p. 120.

if it all?"[278] But Alston thinks Wittgenstein's reasons for accepting certain presuppositions are different from his own, and further accuses Wittgenstein of philosophical illegitimacy, dismissing his views as "unworthy of the name of philosophy."[279]

In "Perceptual Experience, Doxastic Practice, and the Rationality of Religious Commitment," Robert Audi writes that the "basic idea of [Alston's] practice conception . . . is that beliefs are justified or unjustified in relation to some social practice in which certain modes of belief-formation are recognized as conferring justification on the beliefs they generate provided that there are no undermining factors . . . ."[280] Indeed, this is the traditional take on Alston's epistemology, and given this common interpretation, it would be very easy to differentiate Alston's view from Wittgenstein's. But if we look closer, we will find that Alston's view is more sophisticated and subtle than Audi realizes. Alston defines a doxastic practice as

> a system or constellation of *dispositions* or habits, or, to use a currently fashionable term, *mechanisms,* each of which yields a belief as output that is related in a certain way to an 'input'. The sense perceptual doxastic practice . . . is a constellation of habits of forming beliefs in a certain way

---

[278] Alston, Perceiving God: The Epistemology of Religious Experience. Ithaca, NY: Cornell University Press, 1991. p. 150.

[279] Alston, 1989. p. 12.

[280] Audi, Robert. "Perceptual Experience, Doxastic Practice, and the Rationality of Religious Commitment." Journal of Philosophical Research, Volume XX, 1995. p. 7.

on the basis of inputs that consist of sense experiences.[281]

There are a number of subtle differences that might be noticed between Audi's interpretation and Alston's definition, but the one I wish to emphasize presently is that nowhere in his account does Alston mention *justification*. And the omission of this word is indeed crucial. For Alston rejects the idea that the majority of our empirical beliefs are epistemically justified. Rather, he argues for a more philosophically conservative position *that taking these beliefs to be justified and assuming such belief-forming practices as sense perception and memory to be capable of rendering justification, is practically rational.* In "A 'Doxastic Practice' Approach to Epistemology," Alston writes,

> I said . . . that it is rational for us to engage in such practices. Indeed, I claimed that there was no rational alternative to this. It is a kind of practical rationality that is in question here. In reflecting on our own situation – what alternatives are open to us – we come to realize that we are proceeding rationally in forming and evaluating beliefs in ways that are established in our society and that are firmly embedded in our psyches.[282]

And:

---

[281]   Alston, 1989. p. 5.
[282]   Alston, 1991. p. 168.

> I believe that in showing it to be rational
> to engage in [sense perception] I have not
> thereby shown [sense perception] to be
> reliable, but shown it to be rational to
> suppose [it] to be reliable.[283]

The similarities between Wittgenstein's language-games and Alston's doxastic practices are manifest. Wittgenstein maintains that the language-game is something we are brought up into. Alston agrees, writing, "Practice precedes theory; the latter would be impossible without the former."[284] And: "We learn to form perceptual beliefs about the environment in terms of the conceptual scheme we acquire from our society."[285] And again:

> These practices are acquired and engaged
> in well before one is explicitly aware of
> them and critically reflects on them. When
> one arrives at the age of reflection, one
> finds oneself ineluctably involved in their
> exercise.[286]

For Wittgenstein, language-games are unchosen. Alston concurs, saying, "The term 'practice' will be misleading if it is taken to be restricted to voluntary activity; for I do not take belief-formation to be voluntary."[287] Connectedly, Wittgenstein takes his language-games to be social through

---

[283]   ibid. 178; see also 180. Alston repeats these passages nearly
        verbatim in The Reliability of Sense Perception, pp. 130-131.
[284]   ibid. 163.
[285]   ibid. 163.
[286]   Alston, 1989. p. 7.
[287]   ibid. 5.

and through. Again, Alston agrees. "These practices are thoroughly *social*," he writes, "socially established by socially monitored learning, and socially shared."[288] Like language-games, doxastic practices are inherently plural: "On this approach . . . pluralism reigns; there is no common measure for all beliefs. The epistemic status of a particular belief depends on the doxastic practice(s) from which it sprang."[289] Finally, like language-games, doxastic practices are dynamic, not static: "We should not suppose that doxastic practices are immutable. They can and do change."[290] Robert Adams sums this up, writing,

> Rationality is possible for us only through forming and assessing beliefs in ways, or practices, that are socially established and socially learned. These practices, while intimately connected with each other are irreducibly plural, in the sense that they cannot be reduced to any single overarching practice or criterion . . ..[291]

Despite this obvious resemblance, Alston does not consider himself a Wittgensteinian, or as he writes in *The Reliability of Sense Perception*, "If this is Wittgensteinianism, it is a non-verificationist, realist, un-Wittgensteinian form."[292] Throughout his writings, Alston belittles

---

[288] Alston, 1989. p. 8.

[289] ibid. 25.

[290] Alston, 1991. p. 163.

[291] Adams, Robert. "Religious Disagreements and Doxastic Practices." Philosophy and Phenomenological Research, 1994. Volume 54 (4) p. 885.

[292] Alston, 1993. p. 130.

Wittgenstein, continually making two charges against him: that Wittgenstein is a verificationist and that he is an anti-realist. In this section, I will examine these charges and will attempt to defend Wittgenstein against them, showing that he is not a verificationist (in the way that Alston takes him to be) and also not an anti-realist. Let me begin with the charge of verificationism.

Alston accuses Wittgenstein of this epistemic offense in *Perceiving God, The Reliability of Sense Perception,* and on almost every page of "A 'Doxastic Practice' Approach . . .". Here are but a few of the manifold charges:

> Now I do not accept for a moment Wittgenstein's verificationist restrictions on what assertions, questions, and doubts are intelligible.[293]

> I can perfectly well understand the propositions that sense perception is (is not) reliable, that physical objects do (do not) exist, and that the earth has (has not) been in existence for more than a year . . ..[294]

> The concept of a trans- or inter-language-game dimension of truth or falsity is ruled out on verificationist grounds.[295]

> Wittgenstein's linguistic solution, as already pointed out, is that no meaning can be given to a question as to the truth or

---

[293] Alston, 1989. p. 5.

[294] ibid. 5.

[295] Alston, 1991. p. 154.

justifiability of beliefs that are constitutive of a practice.[296]

I have already made clear that I do not accept the verificationist assumptions that underlie Wittgensetin's restrictions on meaningfulness, and hence I cannot avail myself of his solution.[297]

In both [Wittgenstein's language-games and my doxastic practices], there is an emphasis of the indefinite plurality of doxastic practices, their social establishment, their pre-reflective genesis, and their involvement in wider spheres of practice. And in both cases, there is the crucial insistence that, in a sense, there is no appeal beyond the practices we find ourselves engaged in. But that crucial point finds a much more uncompromising expression in Wittgenstein. He holds that there can be no way of subjecting established language-games to rational criticism; and hence, on his verificationist principles, it is meaningless to ask whether such a practice is reliable, or whether its basic presuppositions are true, known, or justifiably believed. I reject both of these claims.[298]

---

[296] Alston, 1989. p. 9.

[297] ibid. 9.

[298] Alston, 1993. p. 130.

I do not mean to belabor the point, but I want to express the depth and bitterness of Alston's attacks with one final quote: (Note also the connection that Alston assumes here between verificationism and anti-realism.)

> Finally, I should mention the point that one reason my account is closer to Reid's is that Reid had the advantage of philosophizing before the advent of *verificationist and other anti-realist philosophies.* Reid never suggests that there is anything unintelligible about the idea that e.g., sense perception is or is not reliable, or that we cannot meaningfully ask the question of whether this is so, however difficult it may be to find a way to answer the question.[299]

It is striking the number of times that Alston repeats this criticism and one naturally questions why Alston is so inordinately preoccupied with this charge of verificationism. Perhaps he was bullied by verificationists as a child. In any case, I am not the first to notice Alston's obsession with verificationism. Richard Gale writes, "No sooner is the 'v' word used than Alston responds by charging its user with being an 'epistemic imperialist' . . .."[300] In addition to his concern about verificationism being excessive, and possibly obsessive, it seems to me that it is also misguided (when aimed against Wittgenstein.)

Wittgenstein is simply not a verificationist. Or more

---

[299]   Alston, 1989. p. 9; italics added.

[300]   Gale, Richard M. "Why Alston's Mystical Doxastic Practice is Subjective." Philosophy and Phenomenological Research, 1994. Volume 54 (4). p. 874.

precisely, he is not a verificationist in the way that Alston believes him to be. To read Wittgenstein as a simple logical positivist is to miss entirely his salient and original contribution to philosophy. Of course, Wittgenstein challenges the meaningfulness of certain questions that Alston takes to be meaningful. But when Wittgenstein does this, he is certainly not objecting that he does not understand the proposition being expressed. Let me illustrate: In the passages quoted above, Alston is clearly charging that Wittgenstein maintains that a question such as *Has the world existed for more than a year?* lacks propositional meaning, is nonsensical or cannot be understood, much like the poorly formed question *Blue trumpet Tuesday Sheila?* But this is not Wittgenstein's point at all. Rather, Wittgenstein suggests that if a person is asking certain skeptical questions, we might have good reason to believe they are failing to understand something fundamental about their situation, or that they are pursuing a question that could not possibly be fruitful. He writes, "If I make certain false statements, it becomes uncertain whether I understand them."[301] And later,

> Why is it not possible for me to doubt that I have never been on the moon? . . . First and foremost, the supposition that perhaps I have been there would strike me as *idle*. Nothing would follow from it, nothing be explained by it. It would not tie in with anything in my life.[302]

---

[301] On Certainty, §81.

[302] ibid. §117.

Plainly Alston is either misunderstanding Wittgenstein or he is equivocating on the notion of verificationism. Richard Gale charges him with the latter, writing,

> It is over this issue that Alston falls into serious equivocation between verificationism as a necessary condition for a sentence's meaningfulness, which I will call 'meaningfulness-verificationism,' and as a necessary condition for a type of experience qualifying as cognitive in virtue of the beliefs based on them being verifiable, which I will call 'cognitivity-verificationism.'[303]

I would not put the distinction exactly the way Gale has, but of course, this is irrelevant. The important point is that both Gale and I find something fishy about Alston's use of and attacks on verificationism. By verificationism, Alston means quite simply the sort of 'meaning-verificationism' associated with the logical positivists, and clearly Wittgenstein does not hold such a position.

This leads me to Alston's second accusation, that Wittgenstein is an anti-realist. By anti-realists, Alston seems to have in mind the same group of philosophers mentioned earlier together with the early pragmatists. In short, he has in mind those who reject the distinction between appearance and reality and/or those who define truth in terms of justification (or verification.) But as I have already shown in Chapter Two, Wittgenstein does not ascribe to these metaphysical commitments. Let's look explicitly now

---

303   Gale, 874.

at how Alston responds to the three defining criteria of epistemic contextualism.

Clearly, as regards the first distinguishing point, Alston agrees with the contextualists. Our most basic empirical beliefs are not epistemically justified, but rather it is practically rational to act as though they are. Alston insists on this distinction unlike the epistemic pragmatists. Second, Alston rejects pragmatist metaphysics, attempting to separate himself from his philosophical antagonist (Wittgenstein) by suggesting that he (Wittgenstein) is an anti-realist who denies a distinction between appearance and reality and between truth and justification. I wish to turn now to one of the most difficult cases to decide, the ever-evolving epistemology of Hilary Putnam.

Section 3.5: Hilary Putnam Considered

Joseph Margolis identifies Hilary Putnam as "the central figure of the 'second generation' [of pragmatists]"[304] In another article, Margolis claims that Putnam is a "self-confessed pragmatist . . ."[305] and later, that "Putnam . . . plainly regards himself as a pragmatist and indeed is a pragmatist . . . ."[306] In this section, I would like to explore Putnam's candidacy for being an epistemic pragmatist according to my distinction. For the purposes of this book, I wish to focus on one specific aspect of Putnam's philosophy, the relationship between truth and justification. Clearly, the Hilary Putnam we meet in 1981's *Reason, Truth, and History* shares deep

---

[304] Joseph Margolis, "Richard Rorty: Philosophy By Other Means," p. 532.

[305] Margolis, "Reconstruction in Pragmatism," p. 231.

[306] ibid. p. 231.

affinities with the classical pragmatists. Like James and Dewey, Putnam here holds that our most basic beliefs are pragmatically justified and that truth is defined in terms of justification. He writes, "the only criterion for what is a fact is what it is *rational* to accept. (I mean this quite literally and across the board; thus if it can be rational to accept that a picture is beautiful, then it can be a *fact* that the picture is beautiful.)"[307] Margolis captures Putnam's early view well, writing: "As a Jamesian pragmatist, Putnam had originally claimed that 'Truth' . . . is some sort of (idealized) rational acceptability . . . and not correspondence with mind-independent or discourse-independent 'states of affairs.' There is [he affirms] no God's Eye point of view of actual persons reflecting various interests and purposes that their descriptions and theories subserve[.]"[308] Putnam continues to hold similar beliefs concerning the commitments of pragmatist metaphysics through 1990, when he published a collection of essays entitled, *Realism With a Human Face*. In the Preface to that volume, he reprises his earlier refrain, saying, "According to my conception, to claim of any statement that it is true, that is, that it is true in its place, in its context, in its conceptual scheme, is, roughly, to claim that *it could be justified were epistemic conditions good enough.*"[309] In this book, he takes care to distinguish his theory of justification from Peirce's:

> Many people have thought that my idealization
> was the same as Peirce's, that what the figure

---

[307] Putnam, Reason, Truth, and History. Cambridge, U. K.: Cambridge University Press, 1981. Preface, p. x.

[308] Margolis, "Reconstruction in Pragmatism," p. 236.

[309] Hilary Putnam, Preface to Realism With a Human Face. Cambridge, MA: Harvard University Press, 1990. p. vii.

of a 'frictionless plane' corresponds to is a situation ('finished science') in which the community would be in a position to justify *every* true statement (and to disconfirm every false one.) People have attributed to me the idea that we can sensibly imagine conditions which are simultaneously ideal for the ascertainment of any truth whatsoever. I have never thought such a thing, and I was, indeed, so far from ever thinking such a thing that it never occurred to me even to warn against this misunderstanding when I wrote *Reason, Truth, and History . . ..*[310]

He continues:

Thus, I do not by any means *ever* mean to use the notion of an 'ideal epistemic situation' in this fantastic (or utopian) Peircian sense. By an ideal epistemic situation I mean something like this: If I say, 'There is a chair in my study,' an ideal epistemic situation would be to be in my study with the lights on or with daylight streaming through the window, with nothing wrong with my eyesight, with an unconfused mind, without having taken drugs or been subjected to hypnosis, and so forth, and to look and see if there is a chair there.[311]

---

[310] ibid. p. vii-viii.
[311] ibid. p. viii.

Although his epistemology is distinct from Peirce's, Putnam, like Peirce, relates truth and justification. He writes, "I am simply denying that we have in any of these areas a notion of truth that totally *outruns* the possibility of justification."[312] At some point in the 1990s, Putnam's views changed however. Margolis tells us that in the Dewey Lectures, Putnam rejects many of his core epistemological and metaphysical views.[313] By the time that he publishes *Pragmatism: An Open Question* in 1995, Putnam is now saying that we need not "follow the pragmatists in identifying the true with what is (or what would be) 'verified' in the long run[,]" and "[u]nlike the pragmatists, I do not believe that truth can be *defined* in terms of verification."[314] I do not fault Putnam as some do for his ever-changing views. One lesson he seems to have learned from his study of the pragmatists is that it is better to allow one's beliefs to evolve than to stubbornly remain static. The meager lesson I wish to draw from the passages above is simply that if Putnam was ever an epistemic pragmatist, he is no more, since he no longer defines truth in terms of justification or verification. Let's close our investigation of some contemporary "neo-pragmatists" with a brief look at the philosophies of Quine and Brandom.

SECTION 3.6: PSEUDO-PRAGMATISTS – QUINE AND BRANDOM

As stated earlier in this chapter, perhaps the first thinker to be referred to as a "neo-pragmatist" was Willard Quine.

---

[312] ibid. ix.

[313] Margolis, 1999. p. 231.

[314] Putnam, 1995. p. 11.

Let's see if this title is deserved by studying two passages of text which are representative of Quine's epistemology. The first is an explication of Quine's "Two Dogmas of Empiricism" by R. J. Richman. The second is a passage directly from Quine's seminal 1951 article:

> Neo-pragmatism views human knowledge as a vast concatenation of statements deductively related, and such that, in effect, the whole system is tested whenever a particular entailed experiential statement is tested. On this account all of our scientific knowledge, including logic, is a conceptual scheme which functions 'ultimately, for predicting future experience in the light of past experiences.' (p. 41)[315] Science is pictured, metaphorically, as a 'field of force whose boundary conditions are experience'. (p. 39) In terms of this metaphor, certain statements are pictured as near the center of the field; others, as near its boundary. Those near the periphery are the ones 'especially germane to particular experiences.' (p. 40) . . . On occasion, experiences different from those predicted on the basis of our conceptual scheme occur. On such occasions we must make revisions somewhere in the 'field' of scientific knowledge.[316]

---

[315] Page references refer to Quine's "Two Dogmas of Empiricism," 1951.

[316] Richman, "Neo-Pragmatism," Methodos, Volume 8, 1956. p. 37.

Quine:

> A conflict with experience at the periphery
> occasions readjustments in the interior
> of the field. Truth-values have to be
> redistributed over some of our statements.
> Re-evaluation of some statements entails re-
> evaluation of others, because of their logical
> interconnections the logical laws being in
> turn simply certain further elements in the
> field. Having re-evaluated one statement we
> must re-evaluate some others, whether they
> be statements logically connected with the
> first or whether they be statements of logical
> connections themselves. But the total field
> is so underdetermined by its boundary
> conditions, experience, that there is much
> latitude of choice as to what statements to
> re-evaluate in light of any single contrary
> experience. No particular experiences are
> linked with any particular statements in
> the interior of the field, except indirectly
> through considerations of equilibrium
> affecting the field as a whole.[317]

The justification scheme outlined in the passages above
does not seem to be very similar to that of the epistemic
pragmatists, who argue that basic beliefs are immediately
justified or unjustified based upon the practical difference
their veracity would make. Nor does it seem very similar to
the epistemic contextualists, who argue that the regress of

---

[317]   Quine, "Two Dogmas of Empiricism." 1951. p. 39f

inferential justification is terminated by contextually basic beliefs, beliefs which are neither justified nor unjustified but provide conditional justification to higher order beliefs. In fact, there don't seem to be any foundational or higher order beliefs at all in the picture Quine gives us. In his epistemology, all beliefs are inferential, are on the same level, and are epistemically justified by the beliefs which surround them. Quine's epistemology is an epistemic coherentism, not a pragmatism or contextualism at all. So why has Quine so long been associated with the movement known as "neo-pragmatism?" I will attempt to answer that question momentarily. First, let us look at another so-called "neo-pragmatist" who, on close inspection, doesn't seem to be espousing an epistemic pragmatism or contextualism either, Robert Brandom.

Robert Brandom's 1994 book, *Making It Explicit,* which is heralded as a cornerstone piece of literature in the neo-pragmatist tradition, is a practical treatise on speech acts and linguistic performances, which may be inspired by, but connects only indirectly if it all with the primary philosophical projects of James and Dewey. So why has it been thrown together with the likes of Rorty, Putnam, Annis, Alston, and Quine and called neo-pragmatism? In his 2000 article, "Richard Rorty: Philosophy By Other Means," Joseph Margolis gives an interesting answer. Margolis places the blame for the miscategorization of philosophers squarely on the shoulders of one man: Richard Rorty. It is Rorty, Margolis charges, that has intentionally contrived this misshapen band of thinkers as "neo-pragmatists." Margolis asserts that Rorty has craftily misread or misrepresented the philosophies of thinkers such as Davidson, Sellars, and Quine. Regarding Davidson, Margolis writes, "Rorty deliberately deforms Davidson's account of truth so that it may be characterized as Jamesian (that is, as pragmatist), although, at the same time, he deforms James's theory so that it will appear hospitable to something akin to Davidson's refusal to treat the theory of truth as *explanatory* of knowledge."[318] And: "The curious thing is that during the period in which Davidson diverges most from Quine along the lines of a leaner orthodoxy, Rorty gymnastically reconciles Davidson's theory of truth . . . with William James's, making Davidson over into a kind of Jamesian (if not a Deweyan) pragmatist – a maneuver Davidson steadfastly refuses to allow."[319] Regarding Sellars, Margolis writes, "Rorty adds Wilfrid Sellars to his list of 'founding fathers' in order, first, to define what he (Rorty) means by the revival of pragmatism and, second, to work out a reconciliation between pragmatism and the leading figures of the analytic movement."[320] "[I]n pressing Sellar's candidacy [as a neo-pragmatist] . . . Rorty ignores the plain fact that Sellars presses the point in the service of a convinced metaphysics of the most unyielding kind."[321] "It's only in a 'Rortyan reading of 'similar' undertakings that Rorty is able to bring Sellars and Quine together . . .."[322] And: "The retrieval of Sellars from the gathering neglect of the guild illustrates very nicely Rorty's sense of inventing the community to which he wishes to belong . . .."[323] And finally, Rorty constructs the group of neo-pragmatists as he "literally recruits allies of mixed and different conviction – muffling philosophical differences for a time, offering a friendly détente of two, facilitating by

---

[318] Margolis, 2000. p. 533.

[319] ibid. 530-1.

[320] ibid. 532.

[321] ibid. 533-4.

[322] ibid. 534.

[323] ibid. 533.

other than philosophical means the effective subversion of hitherto valid sources of canonical resistance."[324]

I am not sure that Margolis is being fair to Rorty, and it is *not* my position in this book that the group of philosophers that are currently being referred to as "neo-pragmatists" is simply a band deliberately and artificially constructed by Richard Rorty to fit his own selfish purposes. I do agree with Joseph Margolis, however, that some philosophers have been labeled in one way or another for reasons other than that they naturally fit into that group. It is my contention that the present group of thinkers commonly referred to as neo-pragmatists are not all deserving of that title and that if my distinction is thoughtfully applied, the situation will become clearer. In this chapter, I have attempted to codify some 20th century thinkers who have been referred to as neo-pragmatists according to the distinction set out in Chapters One and Two. I have judged Richard Rorty to be an epistemic pragmatist; David Annis and William Alston are, I believe, epistemic contextualists. Hilary Putnam may have adhered to the principles of epistemic pragmatism at one time, but his current views should not be considered either epistemic pragmatist or contextualist. Neither should Quine (an epistemic coherentist) or Brandom, who espouses a philosophy of language which may be inspired by the pragmatists but is not directly pragmatist or Wittgensteinian.

---

[324]   ibid. 535.

CONCLUSION

I N THE PRECEDING pages, I have concerned myself primarily with two major distinctions (and several minor ones). The first major distinction (detailed in Chapter One) was between the traditional paradigms of epistemology, foundationalism and coherentism, and what I have dubbed the existential paradigms. The second and perhaps more important distinction (detailed in Chapter Two) is a distinction between two kinds of existential epistemologies, pragmatism and contextualism.

When I began thinking about this project several years ago and when writing the 2002 paper, "Who's a Pragmatist?: Distinguishing Epistemic Pragmatism and Contextualism", which served as this book's inspiration, I unwittingly made two false assumptions. The first was that the distinction between epistemic pragmatism and epistemic contextualism was clean and neat and that if I found the right set of analytic criteria (the essential necessary and sufficient conditions) and if I swung the hammer just right, the distinction would naturally cleave into two like a chunk of galena. This did not happen, but I do not consider my project a failure because of it. I continue to maintain that there is a distinction and that the distinction is an important one despite the fact it is not an easy one to spot. That distinction again is as follows: among the key and distinguishing features of pragmatism are that (1) pragmatists *avoid the regress problem of inferential justification by arguing that our beliefs are immediately justified or unjustified based on the practical difference their veracity would make in life.* (2) Pragmatists hold *that there is no distinction between truth and justification (or that truth is defined in justificatory terms.)* And finally they hold (3), *that there is no distinction between the world and the world as we perceive and interact with it.* Epistemic contextualists, on the other hand, hold these three distinguishing tenets: (A) *the regress of inferential justification is terminated by beliefs which are logically but not epistemically basic, beliefs which lie beyond being epistemically justified or unjustified and supply only contingent justification to the edifice of empirical knowledge.* We call these beliefs contextually basic beliefs. (B) *Contextualists reject the pragmatist idea that there is no distinction between truth and justification – that they are one and the same enterprise.* And (C) *epistemic contextualists reject the pragmatist idea that appearance and reality are indistinct, that reality is the phenomenal.*

The second false assumption I made when starting this project was that after the distinction was fractured just right, the group of philosophers who have so clumsily been gathered together and labeled as "neo-pragmatists" would clearly and cleanly fall in line according my distinction. The final chapter of my book is largely devoted to codifying and sorting out, to the best of my ability, contemporary thinkers who have been referred to as "pragmatists" or "neo-pragmatists", according to my distinction. While I found that Richard Rorty shares the central features of classical pragmatism and that David B. Annis and William Alston seem to be clear examples of epistemic contextualists, I found that some philosophers do not categorize so easily, for example, Hilary Putnam, W. V. Quine, and Robert Brandom. The fact that these philosophers avoid simple categorization is probably one of the signs of their great originality and importance, just as William James, John Dewey, and Ludwig Wittgenstein eluded easy classification for so long. Although some readers will see this codification project as an anti-climactic end to my work, I rather see it as the practical application of my theoretical rule, a rule which I think is generally right and more helpful than not. Classifying theories of knowledge based on their responses to the regress problem of inferential justification, and their treatment of the distinctions between truth and justification and between appearance and reality can help us understand the contributions and the worldviews of major (and minor) epistemologists.

Certainly, there is more work to be done. This small book has merely sketched an outline of three important distinctions but while I believe these distinctions are natural and not gerrymandered from bias, the lines they cut don't seem to be perfect 90 degree angles and many major figures who have been called "neo-pragmatists" don't fit neatly into boxes. Further, this work has not developed or defended a specific pragmatist or contextualist position but rather contented itself to extol the virtues of the existential paradigms generally. I believe epistemic pragmatism and epistemic contextualism are deserving of greater philosophical attention and I hope that my readers will be persuaded that traditional analytic epistemology does not have a monopoly on knowing.

REFERENCES

Adams, Robert. "Religious Disagreements and Doxastic Practices." *Philosophy and Phenomenological Research,* 1994. Volume 54 (4).

Addams, Jane. *Twenty Years at Hull House.* New York: A Signet Classic, 1960.

William P. Alston, "A 'Doxastic Practice' Approach to Epistemology," *Knowledge and Skepticism.* Edited by Marjorie Clay and Keith Lehrer. Boulder, CO: Westview Press, 1989.

-----. *Perceiving God: The Epistemology of Religious Experience.* Ithaca, NY: Cornell University Press, 1991.

-----. *The Reliability of Sense Perception.* Ithica, NY: Cornell University Press, 1993.

Annis, David B. "A Contextualist Theory of Epistemic Justification." *Empirical Knowledge.* Rowman & Littlefield, 1986.

Audi, Robert. "Perceptual Experience, Doxastic Practice, and the Rationality of Religious Commitment." *Journal of Philosophical Research,* Volume XX, 1995.

Ayer, A. J.. *The Problem of Knowledge.* London: MacMillan, 1956.

Bonjour, Laurence. "Can Empirical Knowledge Have a Foundation?" 1978. *Empirical Knowledge.* Rowman & Littlefield, 1986.

-----. "The Coherence Theory of Empirical Knowledge." 1976. *Empirical Knowledge.* Rowman & Littlefield, 1986.

Brandom, Robert, *Making It Explicit.* Cambridge: Harvard University Press, 1994.

-----. *Rorty and His Critics.* Blackwell, 2000.

Camus, Albert. *The Myth of Sisyphus, New York: Vintage International,* Translated by Justin O'Brien, 1983.

Chisholm, Roderick, "The Myth of the Given." 1964. *Empirical Knowledge.* Rowman & Littlefield, 1986.

-----. *Theory of Knowledge,* 2nd edition. Englewood Cliffs, NJ: Prentice Hall, 1977.

Clifford, William. "The Ethics of Belief," from *Lectures and Essays,* reprinted in *Philosophy of Religion: Selected Readings.* Edited by William L. Rowe and William J. Wainwright. Third Edition. Harcourt Brace College Publishers, 1998.

Dewey, John. "A Short Catechism Concerning Truth," 1910. *The Influence of Darwin on Philosophy.* Bloomington: Indiana University Press, 1965.

----. "Development of American Pragmatism" *The Essential Dewey, Volume 1: Pragmatism, Education, and Democracy.* Edited by Hickman and Alexander. Bloomington: Indiana University Press, 1998.

-----. "The Need for a Recovery of Philosophy," 1917. *The Essential Dewey, Volume 1: Pragmatism, Education, and Democracy.* Edited by Hickman and Alexander. Bloomington: Indiana University Press, 1998.

-----. "The Postulate of Immediate Empiricism," 1905. *The Essential Dewey, Volume 1: Pragmatism, Education, and Democracy,* 1998.

-----. *The Quest for Certainty,* 1929; *The Later Works, Volume 4: 1925-1953,* 1988.

Dooley, Patrick Kiaran. *Pragmatism as Humanism: The Philosophy of William James.* Chicago: Nelson-Hall, 1974.

Ewing, A. C. *Idealism: A Critical Survey.* London: 1934.

Gale, Richard M. "Why Alston's Mystical Doxastic Practice is Subjective." *Philosophy and Phenomenological Research,* 1994. Volume 54 (4).

Gettier, Edmund. "Is Justified True Belief Knowledge?" 1963. *Empirical Knowledge.* Rowman & Littlefield, 1986.

Goodman, Russell B. *Wittgenstein and William James,* Cambridge: Cambridge University Press, 2002.

Greco, John. *Putting Skeptics in Their Place.* Cambridge: Cambridge University Press, 2000.

Harman, Gilbert. *Thought.* Princeton, NJ: Princeton University Press, 1973.

James, William, "Essays in Radical Empiricism," *The Writings of William James,* Edited by John J. McDermott. Chicago: University of Chicago Press, 1967.

-----. "Ethical Importance of the Phenomenon of Effort," *The Writings of William James,* Edited by John J. McDermott. Chicago: University of Chicago Press, 1967.

-----. "Pragmatism and Radical Empiricism," 1907. *The Writings of William James,* 1977.

-----. "Pragmatism's Conception of Truth," 1907. *Pragmatism: The Classic Writings.* Edited by Thayer. Indianapolis: Hackett, 1982.

-----. "What Pragmatism Means," 1907. *The Writings of William James,* 1967.

Ketner Kenneth L, "Pragmaticism is an Existentialism?" *Frontiers in American Philosophy, Volume 2,* 1996.

Kripke, Saul. *Wittgenstein on Rules and Private Language.* Cambridge: Harvard, 1982.

Long, Joseph. "Who's a Pragmatist: Distinguishing Epistemic Pragmatism and Contextualism," *The Journal of Speculative Philosophy,* Volume 16, Number 1, 2002.

Margolis, Joseph. "Reconstruction in Pragmatism," *Journal of Speculative Philosophy,* Volume 13, Number 4. 1999.

-----. "Richard Rorty: Philosophy by Other Means", *Journal of Speculative Philosophy,* Volume 13, Number 4. 1999.

McDonald, Hugh. *System and Paradigm.* Forthcoming.

Moser, Paul. "Empirical Knowledge." 1986. *Empirical Knowledge.* Rowman & Littlefield, 1986.

Peirce, Charles S. *Collected Papers,* Vol. 6. Edited by C. Hartshorne and P. Weiss. Harvard, 1965.

John Pollock, *Contemporary Theories of Knowledge.* Rowman & Littlefield, 1986.

Hilary Putnam, *Pragmatism: An Open Question.* Oxford: Blackwell, 1995.

-----. *Realism with a Human Face.* Harvard University Press, 1990.

-----. *Reason, Truth, and History.* Cambridge University Press, 1981.

-----. "Richard Rorty on Reality and Justification," *Rorty and His Critics.* Edited by Robert Brandom, Blackwell, 2000.

Quine, W. V. O. "Two Dogmas of Empiricism." 1951. *Empirical Knowledge.* Rowman & Littlefield, 1986.

R. J. Richman. "Neo-Pragmatism." *Methodos,* Volume 8. 1956.

Rorty, Richard. "Is Truth a Goal of Inquiry? Donald Davidson versus Crispin Wright," 1995. *Truth and Progress,* 1998.

-----. "Universality and Truth," *Rorty and His Critics.* Edited by Robert Brandom, Blackwell, 2000.

Russell, Bertrand. *Philosophical Essays,* 1966. Reprinted by Routledge, 1994.

Sartre, Jean-Paul. "Existentialism is a Humanism," *Existentialism from Dostoevsky to Sartre,* edited by Walter Kaufman. Cleveland: Meridian Books, 1956.

Seigfried, Charlene Haddock, "Pragmatist Metaphysics? Why Terminology Matters", *Transactions of the Charles S. Peirce Society,* Winter 2001. Vol. XXXVII, Number 1.

-----. "The Pragmatist Sieve of Concepts: Description versus Interpretation," *The Journal of Philosophy,* Volume LXXXVII, Number 11, November 1990,

-----. "William James's Phenomenological Methodology," *Journal of the British Society for Phenomenology,* Volume 20, Number 1, January 1989.

-----. *William James's Radical Reconstruction of Philosophy.* State University of New York Press, 1990.

Seigfried, Hans. "Truth and Use." *Synthese* 128. 2001.

Smith, John E. *Purpose and Thought: The Meaning of Pragmatism.* New Haven: Yale University Press, 1978.

Thayer, H. S. *Meaning and Action: A Critical History of Pragmatism.* Indianapolis: Bobbs-Merrill Company, 1968.

Vohra, Ashok. Preface to *Wittgenstein's Philosophy of Mind.* La Salle: Open Court, 1986.

Williams, Michael. *Unnatural Doubts.* Oxford: Blackwell, 1991.

Wittgenstein, Ludwig. *The Blue and Brown Books,* Oxford: Basil Blackwell, 1958.

------. *Culture and Value,* Peter Winch translation. Chicago: University of Chicago Press, 1980.

-----. *On Certainty.* Edited by G. E. M. Anscombe and G.H. von Wright. New York: Harper, 1969.

------. *Philosophical Investigations,* 2nd ed. Oxford: Basil Blackwell, 1958.

Wright, Crispin. "Facts and Certainty," Henriette Hertz Philosophical Lecture for the British Academy, December 1985, published in *Proceedings of the British Academy LXXI.*

Printed in the United States
By Bookmasters